Two Countries

May Yen Ting

Translated By Amelia Fielden

Two Countries
Quadu Press
ISBN-13 978-0-9855609-3-5
Library of Congress Control Number: 2018965348

Printed in the United States of America

Quadu Press
www.quadupress.com
quadupress@gmail.com

Editors
Ling-Erl Ting [丁玲兒]
Warren Wu [吳維倫]

Contents

Figure 1 – Ting Ruey-Iang and Ting Yen May.

May Yen Ting

Editor's Note

Two Countries is the second collection of *tanka* that my mother, Ting Yen May [丁顏梅], composed between 1975 and 1979. Her first collection, *Destiny*, was originally published in 1975 under her mentor/teacher Shiga Mitsuko-sensei's [四賀光子先生] guidance. After Shiga-sensei's passing in 1976, my mother continued writing *tanka* under the guidance of Shiga-sensei's son, Ōta Seikyū-sensei [太田青丘先生] who wrote the foreword for this book. Even though my mother only started composing *tanka* in her mid-60's after retiring from teaching, she was a diligent writer and most grateful to have the best teachers, Shiga-sensei and Ōta-sensei.

The translation of *Two Countries* into English was mainly for the benefit of future generations who are not proficient in Japanese. I am thankful for Amelia Fielden's smooth flowing translation work, and Maki Tomoe-sensei's proofreading of the phrasing of the original Japanese *tanka*. Also, I thank my husband, Kai-Min Wu, for his translation of the foreword and afterword, my daughter, Sharon Wu, for assisting in the book cover design, and my son, Warren Wu, for his efforts in setting up the bilingual layout and the publishing process.

Deep appreciation goes to my siblings, Joyce Marleau, Leland Ting, Elon Ting, and our sister-in-law, Kathy Ting, for their support of the translation of our mother's work as a keepsake for our descendants. *Two Countries* contains the story of Ting Yen May during the Japanese occupation of Taiwan and the periods of uncertainty of Taiwan's status. It is our hope that

vii

through this book, readers will come to know her and appreciate this collection of *tanka* reflecting her unique life experiences under "two countries."

Ling-Erl Ting
December 3, 2018

Foreword

Two *Countries* is the second collection of *tanka* published by our fellow *Chō-On* [潮音] member, Mrs. Ting Yen May, following *Destiny* which was published in 1975. The foreword of *Destiny* was written by my late mother, Shiga Mitsuko. With the author's postscript, the story of how the author joined *Chō-On Sha* was very well explained.

Two and a half years before the Kantō Earthquake, the author was studying at Tokyo Prefectural First Girls' High School [東京府立第一高等女学校, now Hakuō High School (現白鷗高校)], and taking classes from Shiga. After the disastrous quake, she returned to her hometown of Taipei and finished high school there. Then she attended Tokyo Women's Higher Normal College [東京女高師, today's Ochanomizu University (現お茶の水大學)]. Upon graduation, the author again returned to Taipei. With her knowledge of Japanese and her full understanding of Japan, she taught people in Taiwan the same. She also wrote Japanese textbooks for Taiwanese students.

The author found out that Shiga was involved in selecting the *tanka* for the Imperial *Tanka* Meeting and saw some photos of Shiga in Japanese weekly magazines. In 1971 (昭和 [Showa] 46), she joined *Chō-On* and started to formally study *tanka*. Since joining the association, she has never missed turning in her regular assignments. I have taken over the duty of reviewing her *tanka* after the death of Shiga in 1976 (昭和 51).

This time, as she indicated in the last *tanka* of the collection:

> *with wavering gait*
>
> *have we achieved our aim?*
>
> *two people*
>
> *in a three-legged race,*
>
> *fifty years of marriage*

she wanted to commemorate the 50 years of marriage with her husband, Ting Ruey-Iang [丁瑞鋏], by publishing this collection. The author asked me to write a foreword for this collection.

The title of the collection, *Two Countries*, is illustrated directly by two *tanka*:

> *years have passed*
>
> *as I go and come*
>
> *across the Pacific—*
>
> *I wonder where*
>
> *my final resting place will be*

and

> *put bluntly,*
>
> *is this 'sitting on the fence'?*
>
> *I feel guilty*
>
> *picking and choosing*
>
> *between two countries to live in*

Worried about the uncertain future of Taiwan, most of her children had moved to America and were living there, so the author and her husband purchased a house in Portland, Oregon. They made overseas trips to the house to escape the unbearable summer heat of Taiwan. The author sarcastically wrote of her behavior. *Two Countries* does not just stop there. The blood from her ancestors from Fukien Province made her feel uncomfortably wedged between Taiwan and the People's Republic of China. Furthermore, during the formative years of her life, she received her education in Japan. She was Japanese both in body and soul. She was Chinese, but it was quite difficult to wipe out the feeling of being "Japanese" entirely. She was placed in a complex international situation. She wrote her *tanka* with her heart, naturally and honestly. Thus, this collection stands out and apart from others.

Let us try to illustrate the facts mentioned above by reading some of her work:

fearful of brain-washing,

shall I rent temporarily

in the other country

and go on living there

in celebration of my seventy years?

does this 'stranger'

on the hill trail a shadow

like me?

a single gingko is bathed

in the evening sunlight

awake now, but

my heart is still throbbing —

a dream of being helpless

as I'm chased

over a precipice

with a misgiving

I've no way to explain,

I arrive in America

to live quietly

like someone seeking asylum

These *tanka* relate to the two countries, Taiwan and America, but even America, once you lived there,

as a temporary resident

in this great land America,

so tolerant of all,

I see it is an eventful

and complicated country

is not necessarily a paradise without concerns

the small branches

from the garden trees

I cut down

after moving here, over time

will quietly become waste

chewing hard

at the tough mustard greens

planted in summer,

I am considering

the day for my return

though there's nothing

of special concern these days,

something suddenly

prods my heart—is it

misgiving or lonesomeness?

and a feeling of deep reservation.

As to the status of Taiwan, with the dealings among big nations:

the great powers

who have ended up

throwing out Taiwan

so readily

are playing a card game

she deplored, then upon returning to Taiwan,

before I could tell

what they were, I saw

red flowers

trembling against the blue sky

of my home town

she lamented with deep sorrow.

my sleeping kinship consciousness

was suddenly awakened

on the day

when I first trod the soil

of the mainland   (in 1930 I traveled to the mainland)

These *tanka* were written to reflect upon the trip she made in 1930 to mainland China where she was awakened to her ancestry, but the realities of the People's Republic of China are

when women
hold up half the sky
for the sake of men,
they leave off makeup
wear working clothes

when they differ,
irreconcilable enemies
and fellow countrymen
are divided — they flog
even corpses with their theories

yesterday's 'yes'
becomes today's 'no' —
the self-criticism
of old scholars continues
with no days of respite   (Guo Moruo)

which are not quite agreeable.

for my grandchildren
who've come to rely on the taste
of 'Mom's home cooking,'
I add tofu from Chinatown
and yuzu miso paste from Kyoto

dropping in to Tokyo
I'm buffeted
by waves of people—
I too am getting to have
a Japanese face

meeting at the class reunion
after half a century,
we tell each other in detail
about our respective experiences
of recovery from illnesses

at times I question
my own nature—
living in a house
with sliding paper doors,
I compose tanka *absorbedly*

Special attention should be paid to these which exemplify her deeply imbued Japanese culture. Consequently,

I compose tanka
as if carrying out
a religious practice,
earnestly encouraging myself
to do so for the rest of my life

to engage deeply into *tanka* writing is one way to relieve one's uneasiness.

It is not an easy thing to do to engage so deeply into working on *tanka* as a foreigner. Here one can see how her education at a young age greatly affected and influenced her.

> *among the crowds fleeing*
>
> *on the screen is a motor-bike*
>
> *with a whole family*
>
> *on board, that looks like*
>
> *dried sardines tied together*

> *following a woman*
>
> *who holds a babe in her arms,*
>
> *a young boy*
>
> *leading a dog on a rope*
>
> *in the process of escape*

Observing the images of refugees of Vietnam running away from the violent war, deep thoughts about them might only be possible if the author had an image of herself placed in a similar situation.

Two Countries is not only a collection of the author's unique and priceless experiences in a complex international environment;

> *to my son's wife*
>
> *raised in America,*
>
> *it seems strange,*
>
> *this distinction in size*
>
> *between husband and wife tea cups*

old eyes dazzled,

I look up at

my mixed-blood granddaughter

who has brought her boyfriend

along to visit me

it also offers a glimpse into the old and new cross-sections of the human race. And yet, the author engages herself deeply into working on *tanka*,

my happiness, so silly:

a sense of satisfaction

that wells up

when I've hung out to dry

several lines of washing

neither nostalgic for the past,

nor contemplating the future,

for a while I enjoy

the calming effect of

earnestly weeding my lawn

with its blue sky

green prairies, and white houses,

the scenery

from our car window

resembles a child's painting   (Central Oregon)

a memory of my mother

throwing down to me

a shaddock fruit

from the top of the tree – even now

that makes me feel young again

and the depth of her inner peace also gives readers a sudden wake-up call.

Above all, at this latter half of the 20th century, in view of the various complicated events one encounters in the intricate world of *Two Countries*, *Two Countries* is a monumental collection of *tanka*. Without a doubt, from the viewpoint of human history, the collection raises many questions of significance and is a meaningful work. In that sense, it should be read not only by fellow Japanese *tanka* readers, but also by the people of the world through translation, I hope.

I pray for the safety and welfare of the author.

Ōta Seikyū
July 7, 1981
At the Yō-Yō Mountain Villa of *Chō-On Sha*, Kamakura

Figure 2 – Ōta Ayako and Ōta Seikyū at their Kamakura residence.

1975

インドシナ半島

異なれる
陰の手に國
分たれて
殺戮の月日
いつまで續く　　　　　　（ペトナム）

百萬の
難民蟻の
湧くさまに
右往左往す
ニュース畫面に　　　　（主要都市續々陷落）

オートバイに
目刺の如く
全家族
連ね乗るあり
逃亡の群集

赤子抱く
女に添ひ行く
少年は
犬を牽きをり
逃亡途上

The Indochina Peninsula

the country is divided
under the control of differing
powers behind the throne—
how long will it go on,
this night and day carnage   (Vietnam)

like a welling out
of a million refugee ants
they go this way and that
in the news screened
on television   (collapse of the main towns and cities one after another)

among the crowds fleeing
on the screen is a motor-bike
with a whole family
on board, that looks like
dried sardines tied together

following a woman
who holds a babe in her arms,
a young boy
leading a dog on a rope
in the process of escape

雪崩打つ
逃亡の群に
まじれるか
親米派我が
ベトナムの友

逃亡の
潮引きし後に
何起る
遠き彼の地に
思ひを凝らす

戦へと
蔭より支援して
十餘年
今は知らぬと
言ふか大國

米基地の
子らの喚ぶ聲か
際立ちて
高く徹るも
バンコツクの日暮　　（泰國に立寄りし日）

I wonder if she
is caught up in the avalanche
of fleeing crowds,
my Vietnamese friend
who belongs to the pro-American wing

what will arise
in the wake
of this tide of escape?
my thoughts fix
on her faraway land

that great power
which has covertly
for decades
urged and supported the fighting,
will it now claim to know nothing?

do I hear
calls from the children
on US bases —
they're sounding loud and clear
through the Bangkok dusk   (*the day I stopped in Thailand*)

蔣總統逝く

天滂沱と
雷雨降して
一人の
領袖の死を
哭く春の後夜

復國の機を
島に待ち待ちて
四半世紀
巨星墜ちたり
遺志切々と

亂世に
島の安泰
樹てたりと
一人の靈に
千萬ひれ伏す

The Death of President Chiang

the heavens unleashing
torrential rain and thunderbolts
bewail the death
of a respected leader —
after midnight, in spring

waiting, waiting, on the island
for the time to return to the mainland,
after a quarter of a century
a great leader has fallen,
with his passionate intentions

saying that peace
has come to the island
in these times of tumult,
hundreds and thousands
bow to the spirit of one man

春闌けて

日々青む
柿の若葉と
見るうちに
幽けき花芽
あまた吹き出づ

御所柿や
花芽ぽつつりと
まん中に
花托十字に
開き行く見ゆ

春闌けて
心樂しも
家巡る
果樹次ぎ次ぎに
花の咲き出で

葉の蔭に
ふとみつけたり
垂乳根の
乳首と紛ふ
ザボンの青果

Spring Well-advanced

while I'm watching
as day by day young leaves
on the persimmon tree grow green,
many faint flower buds
are shooting out

oh those Gosho *persimmons!*
on the flowers' cross-shaped bases
I can see
some buds opening
little by little

with spring well-advanced
I am rejoicing—
one after another
the fruit trees around my home
are coming out in bloom

suddenly, in leaf shadow
I discovered on the shaddock
green fruits
exactly like the nipples
of a full-breasted mother

一筋の
下り並木路
楓若葉
陽を反射して
いよいよ明るし

溝底の
積れる土に
こぼれ菜種
生ひて畝との
緑を競ふ

見はるかす
青田の果てに
池一つ
朝の光を
集めて白し

雨止みぬ
一谷緑の
上越えて
山鳩の聲
暫し響かふ

down the avenue
lines of maple trees,
their young leaves
reflecting the sun
gradually lightening

spilt onto the earth
mounded at the bottom of a ditch,
canola seeds are growing
rivaling the green colors
on the ridges

green paddy fields
as far as the eye can see,
and at their extremity
a pond shimmering white
in morning's radiance

the rain has stopped —
for the first time in a while
I hear the voices
of mountain doves calling
through the valley's greenery

友來訪

向ひゐる
初見の友を
<small>しよけん</small>
いやまして
優しく見する
明るき笑まひ　　　　　　　　　　　（潮音同人井いつよ様）

社友とふ
縁に一見
舊知の如
幾日續けし
我らの語らひ

A Friend Comes to Visit

seated opposite is someone
who at first sight
I'll add to my friends —
she looks so nice, and
has a bright smile   (Ino Itsuyo-sama, a fellow Chō-On member)

though our connection
was as colleagues,
this is like an old friendship —
our conversation continued
for days and days

折々に

旅立たせし
子に似て
發送の詠草を
心に幾日
反芻しをり

安らけき
日々にをりつつ
時にふと
胸よぎり行く
一つの空しさ

動亂の
世に事なくて
ある我を
又なき幸と
心足らはん

From Time to Time

it's like a child
made to set out on a journey—
for several days
pondering in my mind
that tanka *manuscript I've sent off*

while I'm enjoying
day after day of relaxation,
at times
a certain emptiness suddenly
flits through my heart

in this unsettled world
I, who am lucky
to be trouble-free,
should feel satisfied
with my matchless good fortune

散歩

脚弱る
自意識よりか
目覺むれば
散歩散歩と
夫は急き立つ

雨風にも
行く早朝の
散策よ
老いひたすらの
修業の如く

屋根にゐる
日曜大工の
^{あるじ}
主人にも
聲を掛けたり
散策の道

心ふと
幼時を思ふ
散歩道
芋買ひて夫と
食べ食べ行けば

16

Taking a Walk

is he self-conscious
about his legs weakening?
as soon as I wake
"let's walk, walk"
my husband urges me

our practice of walking
in the early mornings,
even in rain or wind,
like an earnest ritual
of old age

from the path
we hailed a householder
working on his roof
as a 'Sunday carpenter,'
while we walked

suddenly a youthful memory:
buying sweet potatoes
on our walk,
my husband and I
munching as we go along

負ひ目

女卑家風
初孫(うひまご)我を
いらぬ意に
祖母梅の字音もて
名づけたりしか　　　　　　　（梅の俗音"不要"の臺灣語音に近し）

いらぬ意に
祖母つけし名と
知りてより
梅の我が名に
負ひ目持ちたり

いらぬ嬰女(みどりご)
我の肥立てば
祖母愛でて
臨終までも
我を求めしと　　　　　　　（祖母我が幼時に死す）

18

The Burden

females inferior, a family tradition —
did my grandmother name me,
her first grandchild,
using 'plum' because
it sounds like 'unwanted'?   (the colloquial pronunciation of 'plum' is close to the
Taiwanese word for 'unwanted')

once I realized the name
conferred by Grandmother
can mean 'unwanted,'
I was burdened
with my 'plum' name

as I grew
my grandmother loved me,
this 'unwanted girl'…
she asked for me
to the very end of her life   (Grandmother died when I was still young)

周邊

湯宿より
夜々來る唄を
催眠の
樂と早寢の
床に聽きたり

競ふがに
己が歌をば
聲上げて
歌ひたり
兵の狂院の朝

狂院の
窓の格子に
顏つけて
目を凝らしゐる
兵いつ來て見ても

My Surroundings

going to bed early
and listening to the songs
carried every night
from the hot spring inn,
a hypnotic pleasure

as if competing
they sing individual songs
with loud voices,
soldiers at the asylum
in the mornings

whenever I come here
I see soldiers
staring out
from the asylum windows,
their faces pressed to the grates

七十路

胸突八丁
い行く旅路の
覺束なや
これより向ふ
七十の我が生

百歳は
問題なしと
言ひ放つ
義兄九十四の
顔を目守る

日中條約

覇權とふ
一項にて釘
打たるるか
大國谷間の
國の搖らめき　　　　　（條約中の覇權項目）

The Road to Seventy

so uncertain this path,

steep and perilous,

I have to travel

from now on facing life

in my seventies

I gaze fondly at the face

of my brother-in-law,

now ninety-four, who

declares that getting to a hundred

will be no problem for him

The Japan-China Treaty

will they pound in the nail

with 'domination'

as one of the clauses?

the supreme powers wavering

over this country of valleys   *(the hegemony clause in the treaty)*

渡米

居住權
保持に米國
年參よ
老軀ひつ提げて
何時まで續く　　　　　　　　　（規定により年に一囘の渡米）

長留守の
我が家を鳥ら
占めるしか
軒に作れる
巢は念入りに

明け方の
裏藪に鳴く
鳥の聲
まだ幼なきを
床に聞きをり

May Yen Ting

Visiting the United States

how long can I continue
pushing my old body
to make this annual visit
to the US for the sake of
retaining my resident's visa?   (as per regulation, I go to America once a year)

did the birds
occupy this house
during my long absence?
under the eaves are nests
made with such care

from my bed
I'm listening to the birds,
their still young voices
singing at dawn
in the thicket behind

歌書おきて
西日遮る
楓葉の
輝く緑
時に見やりつ

父親の
好むトマトを
植ゑんとて
庭土起す子の
慣れぬ手つき

二十本の
トマト苗の列
生ひ育ち
白き垣に色
映えて倚り添ふ

アメリカに
住みて老い身を
試さんと
屋根衝く松に
密かに登りぬ　　　　　　　（園丁なかなか来ねば）

putting down
my poetry book, I gazed out
at the green brilliance
of maple leaves
blocking the western sun

intending to plant
the tomatoes favored by his father,
how awkward is our son
unaccustomed to such work
lifting earth in the garden

growing tomato plants,
twenty in a row
their colors
reflected in the white fence
against which they lean

living in America
I tested my old body
by climbing, in secret,
a pine tree
that pokes at the roof   *(the gardener never seems to turn up)*

茂みに身を
隠し女われ
庿衝く
老松ケ枝を
鋸もて切る

少女の日
體操の時の
綱登り
師に褒められしを
憶ひ出でをり

<ruby>車<rt>カー</rt></ruby>王國
我が徒歩利くは
ハイウエイに
取り圍まれし
一小區域

遅れ咲く
庭の幽けき
菜の花に
今日も蝶舞へり
白き陽の中

I, the woman
who hid in their foliage,
with a saw cut off
branches of the old pine
poking at the eaves

I'm remembering that
when I was a young girl
my gym teacher
praised me for my ability
at rope climbing

in this country
where the car is king,
I can walk effectively
only in a small domain
surrounded by highways

on the pale flowers
of late-blooming mustard plants
in my garden
today, too, butterflies dance
in the white sunlight

花とりどり
外に植ゑ置き
戸はひたと
閉ぢてあり丘の
住宅區域

蒲公英の
花絮流るるがに
視野に來て
暫したゆたふ
野の夕明り

孫ら

老い侘ぶる
心の色に
出でにしか
孫は祖母我を
悲しげと言ふ　　　　　　　（五歳の孫娘）

世代の言葉
國情の差異
反抗期の
孫に焦慮して
對話斷えるる

all kinds of flowers
are planted outside, but
the doors of houses
in this hilly residential area
remain firmly shut

just like the fluff
which wafts from dandelions,
the evening light
comes into view for a while
wavering over the field

My Grandchildren

did my heart appear
to be tinged with the worries
of old age?
my granddaughter says she's sad
about me, her grandmother   *(my five-year-old granddaughter)*

generational language
difference in national sentiments —
impatient with my grandchildren
in their rebellious phase,
I'm abstaining from dialogue

後日我を
偲ぶ日もあれ
針毎に
心籠め縫ふ
孫へのコート

孫らとの
つきあひ今は
幾何ぞ
祖母われ唯々と
ゲームの負け役に

幼な孫
心得し如く
叶はざる
ねだりをひそと
我に試む

秋の兆し

青空に
花より紅く
楓の葉
映えをり丘は
既に秋なり

may they remember me
in days to come—
I sew a coat
for my grandchild
with love in every stitch

how much longer now
shall I be able to play
with my grandchildren?
as grandmother, I
willingly lose at our games

as if understanding
it's too much to ask,
my young grandchild
tries pestering me
in whispers

Signs of Autumn

in the blue sky
reflections of scarlet maple leaves
more vivid than flowers—
it is already autumn
on the hill-top

庭木立
いつか鶇_{つぐみ}の
聲絶えて
さやぐ葉群_{むら}に
陽照り柔か

明け方の
庭の薄明り
白き猫
一つ芝生を
よぎりて行きぬ

クレター湖行

樅林
分かつ一線の
果ては空に
ひた走り行く
クレター湖_{レーク}への道

二百年
經しとふ水は
底深く
碧_{あを}く凝りるて
新らしクレター湖

unaware when the voices
of thrushes faded
from trees in my garden,
I hear leaves rustling
under the soft sunlight

dawn:
in the garden's
faint light
a white cat
was crossing the lawn

Trip to Crater Lake

at the end of the line
that bisects the silver fir forest
and runs straight to the sky,
there should be
a path to Crater Lake

water said to have been there
for the past two hundred years
deep-bottomed, blue,
concentrated and still—
natural, this Crater Lake

アメリカの女性達

男友達に _{ボーイフレンド}
孫訪問を
切り上げしと
爽やかに言ふ
アメリカの未亡人

老人に
長き一日よ
行く先は
ロイドセンター
皆ふらつく足に　　　　　　　（ショッピングセンター）

着飾れる
老女ら三々
五々の色
さし添へて行く
ロイドセンターの秋

見聴き食べ
憩ふ諸々 _{もろもろ}
備はりて
老らは一日
ここに倦まざり

36

May Yen Ting

American Women

the American widow
tells me composedly
she cut short
a visit to her granddaughter,
when the girl's boyfriend came

it's a long day
for old people—
we head now
for the Lloyd Center,
all staggering along   *(a shopping center)*

ornately dressed
old ladies, in threes and fives
go round the Lloyd Center
adding more colors
to the autumn

we look, listen, eat,
then rest – everything
is arranged
for us oldies to spend the day
without getting bored here

女性解放の
時代か路傍の
人垣に
大統領を
撃つ女人あり　　　　　（フォード大統領）

持てる國

ストライキを
取締る任務
忘れしか
自がストライキに
入る米警官ら

日々ニュースが
告ぐる 油、瓦斯の
語の數よ
石油ショック續く
この持てる國

自他共に
許す大國
アメリカに
假り住み見れば
多事多端の國

is it the era
of 'Women's Lib'?
in the roadside crowd
there is a woman
attacking the President   *(President Ford)*

The Wealthy Country

have they forgotten
their responsibility
to control strikes,
these American police
who are striking themselves?

daily news reports
carry a number of words
like oil and gas —
the oil shock continues
in this wealthy country

as a temporary resident
in this great land America,
so tolerant of all,
I see it is an eventful
and complicated country

相次ぎし
ビッグニュースに
夫は新聞に
英語學習
兼ねて没頭す

姪の終焉

花の棺に
姪永眠す
我が婚に
附き添ひし日の
乙女の顔に　　　　　　　　（姪アメリカに客死す）

白磁なる
湯舟に沈みて
描く我が
肉體の形骸化
自虐にも似る

with major news items
following one after another,
my husband
absorbs himself in the papers,
improving his English at the same time

My Niece's Death

my niece sleeps
the eternal sleep
in a flower-filled coffin
her face that of the young maid
at my wedding   *(my niece died abroad, in America)*

contemplating
the deteriorating outlines
of my body sunk
in a white porcelain bathtub,
is a kind of masochism

歸臺の途、ハワイにて

二世ドライバー
故國で物せし
巻舌か
ハワイの町の
説明聞かす

ワイキキ濱の
食堂なべて
掲げるる
「故里の味」
とふ日本文字

ギターの音
客のさざめき
濱に滿つ
向ふ水平
殘照の色

May Yen Ting

In Hawaii, on the Way Back to Taiwan

that speech-trill of our driver,
a second generation Japanese migrant…
I wonder if he gained it
in this country – we listen
to his explanation of Hawaiian towns

at Waikiki beach
all the cafés
have signs saying
'the tastes of home,'
in Japanese script

guitar music and
the murmur of customers
suffuse the beach —
beyond, on the horizon
the last colors of the sun

日本にて 鎌倉

鎌倉の
由緒ある谷
扇ケ谷に
我が師いまして
この道一筋に

師らに今日
見ゆる坂ぞ
登り來て
椿の下に
息整へぬ

階一つ
降りては門に
立ちいます
師を振り返り
山荘を辭す

In Japan: Kamakura

my teacher is living
in the historic valley of Kamakura,
Ōgigayatsu,
and I'll follow this path
straight to her place

today I climbed
the slope to visit
my teacher,
breathing steadily
beneath the camellias

going down a step
she stands at the gate —
waving back at my teacher
I bid farewell
to the mountain villa

箱根山

斑らにも
朱紅の紅葉
一山を
取り巻きて視野
とみに明るし

眼に収め
カメラに収めて
箱根山
一山の紅葉を
我が物とせし

箱根山
繰り出でし<ruby>車<rt>カー</rt></ruby>の
列にゐて
天下の険を
眼に捉へんとす

May Yen Ting

Hakone Mountain

the whole mountain
is patched with maple leaves,
crimson and scarlet —
my field of vision is
suddenly bright and clear

gathered in my eyes,
gathered in my camera,
Hakone's mountain
of scarlet leaves
now belongs to me

from our car
in the stream of vehicles
heading for Hakone Mountain,
we try to catch a glimpse
of 'the steepest slopes in the world'

五湖巡り
雲の中なる
富士に眼を
あて行きにつつ
晴間を期待す

抜け出でて
石階の落葉
そと掃きぬ
友の山家に
一夜宿りて

百年紀念祭

馳せ参ぜし
友ら母校と
共に古り
互みに舊^{もと}の
面ざし探る

（お茶の水女子大學）

focused on Mt. Fuji
now hidden among the clouds
around the Five Lakes,
our hope as we go along
is for a break in the weather

slipping away from the house,
I carefully swept fallen leaves
from the stone steps,
when I stayed overnight
at my friend's mountain place

Centenary Celebrations

we mates who've come together
have aged, just like
our alma mater...
we look for traces of the old days
in each other's faces   *(Ochanomizu Women's University)*

機上に

師も友も
紅葉も訪ね
帰途飛機の
右に思はぬ
富士の見送り

靄中の
日本列島を
富嶽一つ
負ひるる如く
天空に顯つ

衆は寡に
敵せずの世か
ハイジャックも
ストもひたすら
被害者となり

May Yen Ting

On the Flight

I visit my teacher, my friends,
and the autumn leaves —
returning home,
on the right side of the plane
an unexpected farewell from Mt. Fuji

through the mist
the scene in the heavens
appeared as if
Mt. Fuji bore on its back
the Japanese archipelago

is this a world
where the majority does not
turn against the minority?
both hijackers and strikers
are truly victimized

陵墓に

陵墓への
長列に佇ち
一池の
白睡蓮に
眼_{まなこ}を放つ   （故蔣總統）

何處より
繰り出で來しか
陵寢に
民ら音なく
一隊又一隊

凪に
騒ぐ楓樹の
向ふ空に
光收めし
大き沒りつ日

May Yen Ting

At the Illustrious Tomb

while I stand in the long queue

for the illustrious tomb,

my gaze turns

to the white water lilies

on a pond   *(the late President Chiang)*

where have they come from?

at the sarcophagus

people stand silently

in one group, then

another group

beyond the maple trees

rustling noisily

in the wintry wind,

a great sun is sinking

with the last light in the sky

1976

送舊迎新

青芝に
散りたる梅の
花びらは
掃かずに年の
大掃除を終ふ

ジャンボ機賣り
ホテルに在る子に
大年の
佳肴を盛りて
夫が届けぬ　　　　　　　　（ボーイングに勤むる次男）

持ち越せし
息災を年の
めでたさに
高年齡の
層に我入る

精進に
誦經三昧の
跡追はず
母の享年
我旣に過ぐ

56

May Yen Ting

'Out With the Old, In With the New'

without sweeping away
the petals scattered
on the green lawn
from our plum trees, I complete
the year-end's big clean up

my husband delivered,
a heap of New Year delicacies
for him, to the hotel
where he's staying,
the son who sells jumbo jets   (our second son, who works for Boeing)

grateful
for getting through another year
unscathed,
I go up a level
to that of great old age

without following
her devotion to religion
and sutra reading,
I am already past the age
Mother was when she died

子らの家
巡り行きつつ
老い母は
自が確かなる
場失ひをりし

純多摩の
名に附されたり
「故」といふ字
思ひ巡らせて
哀傷幾日　　　　　　　　（刑に服せし潮音社友）

今日明日の
命ひたすら
歌に籠め
遺詠の思ひ
花鳥に托す

さ庭

種よりを
見守り來し日よ
鴇色に
山茶花咲きて
我が庭明るし　　　　　　（十年前日本の友より種送らる）

as she made the rounds
of her children's homes,
my old mother
lost a definite place
to call her own

seeing the word 'late'
in front of his pseudonym,
Sumitama,
made me reflect sadly
for several days, on the poet   (*a colleague from the* Chō-On *society who served time in prison*)

living one day at a time,
he devotes himself to tanka —
flowers and birds made themes
for these compositions
he will leave behind

Small Garden

oh, the days I've watched for them
since sowing their seeds...
pink-colored
my sasanqua in bloom
are brightening my garden   (*I was given those seeds ten years ago by a Japanese friend*)

年始客に
山茶花の色
褒めさせて
後一くさり
種のいはれ説く

散り果てし
梅に隣りて
玉椿
去年今年の
花咲き盛る

一樹目に
沁み入るばかり
葉を擴げ
咲き静まれる
玉椿かな

二月早や
一夜の雨に
含み來し
柿の芽尖（さき）は
皆天を指す

I let the New Year guests
compliment me on the color
of my sasanqua,
then I explained at length
the history of the seeds

adjoining the plum trees
which have scattered
all their flowers,
my precious camellia
last year and this, bloomed abundantly

how impressive,
the way this tree spreads out
its leaves —
standing calmly in bloom
ah, my precious camellia

though it's still February,
on the persimmon tree
soaked by a night's rain
the tips of the buds are
all pointing at the sky

ザボンの木
仰ぎて蕾
確かむる
我を小猫の
眩しみ見るも

獨り居の
我が窓外に
小鳥たち
話しかくれば
耳立てて聽く

我に物
告げてゐるらし
鳥の聲
姿見えねど
懇ろに聽く

朝來ては
よき音聞かする
鳥の業か
木の上のパパイヤ
實は皆虛ろに

I'm looking up
at the shaddock tree
to check its buds—
the little cat watches me
in a dazzle of sunlight

I live alone,
and when the little birds
come chattering
outside the windows,
I prick up my ears to listen

these bird cries,
it's as if they are trying
to tell me something—
though I can't see them
I listen carefully

coming in the mornings
to make lovely sounds, is
the birds' work, perhaps—
all the papayas
on the tree are hollow

二つ三つ

鳴き出でかかり

後(しり)切れぬ

蛙初聲

いたく幼し

春

天邊より

縞目の如く

鋤の跡

下し來れる

峽の春耕

なだらかな

木の背に靜まる

白鷺ら

野の高き陽に

まだ覺めぬらし

目路の限り

植付けを待つ

田の面に

日光(て)りて天地

今一色に

after giving
two or three croaks,
they've stopped completely —
painfully young
those frogs' first cries

Spring

from high in the sky
they look like stripes, those marks
left by ploughs
turning the earth
in the spring gorges

by a tree with gently curved back,
white herons motionless
and silent, as if
not yet woken by the sun
high over the fields

as far as I can see
stretch paddy fields waiting
to be planted…
on their surface sun glittering,
heaven and earth now one color

枯芒
踏みしだかれて
一しきり
匂ひ噴き上ぐ
丘の細道

貰ひ水
桶満つるまで
屈まりて
烟草燻らす
老い獨り者

老兵の
影見えずなりて
手植ゑし菜
雑草の蔭に
僅か残りぬ

雨後

一谷を
埋むる緑
色まして
雨後の朝陽に
匂ふばかりに

for a while
the scent of trampled
withered, pampas grass
wafts up, drifting
over the narrow hill path

until he gets enough water
to fill his bucket,
the old loner
is crouched down
smoking a cigarette

the old soldier
has disappeared from view —
only a little remains
in the shade, of the greens
he planted by hand

After the Rain

a valley filled
with deepening green…
in the morning sun
after rain
stunningly lovely

下り道
楓並木の
芽ぐみ來て
雨後の日影に
烟りて見ゆる

近くて遠き大陸の國

眠りゐる
血の意識ふと
覺まされつ
大陸の土
初めて踏みし日 　　　　　　　（一九三〇年に大陸に旅す）

武力に
我が歸屬逼^せめんか
大陸の
ニュース一々に
心集むる

曽野女史の
大陸の手記
讀み讀みて
我が描かんとす
中國のイメージ

maple trees

lining the road down the hill

have come out in bud;

in the sunlight after rain

they seem to be smoldering

The Near and Yet Distant Mainland

my sleeping kinship consciousness

was suddenly awakened

on the day

when I first trod the soil

of the mainland   *(in 1930 I traveled to the mainland)*

with military might

do they force us

to belong?

news from the mainland

is increasingly of concern

reading, reading more

of the memoranda

about the mainland

by Mrs. Sono, I try

to draw images of China

膳立てし
聞かせ見せ用の
プログラムに
大陸の實體
なほ　幕（カーテン）の中

鎮座して
大小國の
首領らの
參上を受く
摩訶不思議力

革命の
荒療治もて
蔑視されし
民族の誇り
取り戻せしか

恐れつつ
慇懃に氣を
遣ふなり
曽て眠れる
獅子と侮りし

in the program set up
for the purpose of telling
and showing us things,
the actual state of the mainland
remains behind a curtain

sitting in state
they receive formal visits
from the leaders
of large and small nations —
such great and mysterious powers

subsequent
to the drastic dealings
during the revolution,
when they were treated with contempt,
did the people get back their pride?

though fearing China
they handle her so courteously —
formerly, this country
was scorned and compared
to a sleeping lion dog

ニクソン大統領訪中の時、毛主席身邊の痰壺洋人の興味を引き、香港の店の痰壺忽ち賣れね

仰がるれば
その痰壺も
眞似られて
忽ちブームを
捲き起したり

子供らは
鸚鵡となりしか
毛主席
親より好きと
タテマへを言ふ

女らは
天の半分
支ふれば
男の爲に
粧はずとナツパ服

怕れ持つ
民とやなりし
外人の
友好微笑に
視線をそらす

May Yen Ting

At the time of President Nixon's visit to China, the spittoon which Chairman Mao kept by his side attracted the interest of Westerners, whereupon this type of spittoon sold out in Hong Kong shops.

once he was

so highly regarded

even his spittoon

was copied, suddenly

booming in popularity

have children

turned into parrots?

they mouth theories,

say they love Mao Tse-Tung

more than their parents

when women

hold up half the sky

for the sake of men,

they leave off makeup

wear working clothes

we have become

a fearful people,

withdrawing our gaze

from the smiles of friendship

offered by outsiders

八億の
民個々の聲は
聞えずて
大群の
青 蟻となり果つ

革命の
歴史重ねに
重ねきて
未だ住むに嚴し
中華とふ國

我が經て來し
戰中の日の
幾倍か
嚴しさに堪へん
大陸の民

見解異なりても友人たり得ると訪問團に鄧副總理の言ふ

意見の差異も
友たり得ると
國人の
爲にあらざり
鬭爭續く

with the individual voices
of eight hundred million people
unable to be heard,
they have ended up conforming
in a huge swarm of blue ants

China, still a country
in which living is harsh,
with revolution
after revolution, happening
throughout its history

how many times
the amount of hardship
we experienced during the war
will the people of the mainland
have to endure?

Vice Premier Deng says on his visit that we can be friends, even if we have differing points of view.

even if opinions differ
friendship is possible,
so he says,
yet against the people's interests
the struggle continues

異なれば
不倶戴天と
同胞ら
分かれて死屍にも
鞭打つイズム

昨日の是^ぜ
今日は非となる
老學者
自己批判續き
寧日もなし　　　　　　（郭沫若）

古き世へ
國逆行して
汚染なし
噪音聞かずや
北京の好日

海外の
子よりの外貨
嘉されて
叔母極權下に
今安泰と　　　　（海外の仕送りある者優遇さる）

76

when they differ,
irreconcilable enemies
and fellow countrymen
are divided—they flog
even corpses with their theories

yesterday's 'yes'
becomes today's 'no'—
the self-criticism
of old scholars continues
with no days of respite (Guo Moruo)

reverting to the old world,
the nation has no pollution,
no cacophony
of noise—fine days
in Beijing

the foreign currency
received from her children overseas,
is much appreciated
by my aunt, now secure
even in extremity (people with remittances from overseas are welcomed)

曽野綾子女史の中國訪問手記により想を起す…されど

同胞の
（はらから）

牆に閲ぐか
（かき）（せめ）

聲上げて

相手の非鳴らす

身の後ろめたさ

ロッキード事件

短日を

惜しみるつつも

讀み次ぎぬ

日本紙上の

ロッキード事件

霧の中の

正體はいつ

露るる
（あらは）

固唾を呑みて

新聞をおく

Some thoughts provoked by the memoranda written about her visit to China by Ms. Sono Ayako... nevertheless

> *do fellow countrymen*
>
> *blame each other for the barrier*
>
> *between them?*
>
> *loudly each declaims the other's faults,*
>
> *despite his own guilty conscience*

The Lockheed Incident

> *while I was regretting*
>
> *the shortness of the days,*
>
> *I continued reading*
>
> *about the Lockheed incident*
>
> *in the Japanese newspapers*
>
> *when*
>
> *will the fog clear*
>
> *and the truth emerge?*
>
> *with a lump in my throat*
>
> *I put the newspaper down*

憂國の
士とふ隱れ蓑
剝がるると
潛り行きしか
病院の門

衆人の
環視怒號に
救急の
擔架の上や
針の筵なる

病む床に
如何に聽きるん
己が世の
事洗はれて
莫逆訊さる

did he escape
through the hospital gates,
afraid of being stripped
of his disguise
as a patriotic warrior?

all eyes fixed
angrily on him, he was
taken by ambulance
lying on a stretcher —
a bed of nails, that was

from his sickbed
how will he hear about
the affairs of his world
being investigated,
his firm friendships probed

しやがの花

白む日に
胡蝶花の脹らみ
極まりて
擬寶珠となりし
一瞬に出逢ふ

含み來て
放ちたる胡蝶花
一片に
諸葉搖らぎぬ
庭の明時

湧き出でし
群蝶の舞か
しやがの花
朝の木蔭に
白々と咲く

ブーム消えし
拓地おのづから
なる營みか
幾春過ぎて
もとの原野に

'Shaga' Flowers

as the day lightens,
I witness the moment
a shaga *iris bud*
swells to become the shape
of a bulbous bridge ornament

the shaga *iris has swollen*
and released its flower —
a single petal
is stirring all the leaves
in my dawn garden

are they butterflies
swirling up to dance,
these iris flowers
blooming whitely
in the shade of morning trees

how many springs did it take,
after the boom ended,
for nature itself
to return to wild fields
the land cleared for development?

四賀師を哭く

我が視線
一瞬揺らぎぬ
息呑みて
師の訃紙上に
繰返し讀む

八月に
會はんと書きて
賜びし
書^{ふみ}温もりもちて
今届きしに

今日ぞ師の
み葬り
心馳せ行きて
身は涙人^{るいじん}と
我がなり果てつ

教へ賜びし
この道よ今日
師を悼む
涙先立ちて
筆は進まず

May Yen Ting

Mourning Teacher Shiga

reading over and over
the paper announcing
my teacher's death,
momentarily my sight blurred
and I swallowed hard

today I was honored
with a letter from her —
filled with warmth,
it said we would meet
in August

it is today,
the funeral of my teacher —
I rush to attend
in my mind, but my body
remains here, weeping

oh, this Way that she taught me —
today mourning
for my teacher
tears come first, and I make
no progress with my pen

生死

生きの身の
老い來ていよよ
堪へがたく
聞くも誰逝き
誰病める事

何かすべき
事ある如し
今死なば
少し困ると
胸の底に聲

疎まれて
死んだがましと
酒亂の子
まこと死ぬれば
哀れ殘りぬ　　　　　　　（ある身内の子）

Life and Death

as I live,
my body is aging—
it becomes harder and harder
to bear, hearing of this one dying
and that one ailing

seemingly
there is something I must do—
a voice deep in my heart
tells me if I die now
there'll be a slight problem

best for me
to die shunned, says
the drunken son—
it would be pitiful
were he really to die   *(a certain relative's child)*

仰ぎ見る

鳩群の
旋囘の後
鷹一つ
受けてゆつたり
舞ふ空の高きに

九十九折り
峡の細路を
白き蝶
よろばひにつつ
我を抜き行く

仰ぎては
數へ見る柿
一樹の實
未だにしかと
その數知らず

May Yen Ting

Gazing Up

after a flock of doves
goes swirling past
high in the sky
in turn comes a hawk
to perform its leisurely dance

as I lurch around
the ninety-nine bends
of the ravine's narrow road,
white butterflies
are overtaking me

gazing up, gazing up,
I try counting them,
but I still don't know
for sure how many persimmons
are on that one tree

朝庭に
柿の實數ふる
他愛なさ
今の時點の
幸と思はん

巢立ちたる
雀の子らし
萱の葉に
乘りては落つる
羽ばたき頻りに

時じくの
蟲の音荒屋を
取りまきて
一際高し
朝行くこの道

<ruby>煩<rt>うるさ</rt></ruby>くは
なきかと<ruby>都市<rt>まち</rt></ruby>の
子が問へり
丘の我が家は
降る蟬時雨

May Yen Ting

in the morning garden
I count the fruit
on the persimmon tree —
at this point in time
I think of silliness as a blessing

endlessly getting on
the kaya grass leaves, then
falling off again
flapping their wings, they look like
baby sparrows who've left the nest

the perpetual clamor
of insects surrounding
the ruined house
is noticeably louder, when I
walk this path in the mornings

children in the town
asked whether it wasn't noisy
at my hill-top house
with the cicadas chirring
like showers of rain

懐古

寮庭の
立葵咲き
上り行けば
そぞろ急かれし
帰郷の心　　　　　　　　　　（お茶の水學寮の暑暇）

幼な手を
引かれ峠に
初めて見し
海のその碧^{あを}
今も目に顯つ

May Yen Ting

Recalling the Old Days

when hollyhocks bloomed higher

in the dormitory garden,

my heart could not wait

to hasten home

to my birthplace   (*summer vacation at the residence hall of Ochanomizu University*)

even now I can see

the blue of the ocean

I first gazed upon,

when taken by my young hand

to the top of the hill

孫らの歸省

死んだ人
もう見えぬにと
四つの孫
靈柩の花
怪しみ言ふも

七年間
マミーに支配
され來しと
七つになれる
孫の言ひ分

順ぐりに
仕ふる如く
己が子に
振舞ふ我ら
三代の集ひ

老い二人
張り切りて後
くたびれぬ
孫ら來てよし
引揚げてよし

May Yen Ting

My Grandchildren Return to Taiwan

dead people
can't see any more, says
my four-year-old grandchild,
suspiciously, looking
at the flowers on the coffin

turning seven
my grandchild complains
she has been
under the control of 'Mommy'
for seven whole years

at our three-generation
family gathering,
I behave
towards my own children
as if attending them in order

we two oldies,
at first excited, then exhausted —
it's great when
grandchildren come to visit,
great when they go home

潮音全國大會（第十三囘）

今一度
師よ目覺めませ
大會に
みあとつがんと
我ここにあり　　　　　　　　（東慶寺御墓前に）

師の御影
求<small>と</small>めん心に
山莊をも
とほれば香<small>かう</small>
仄かに匂ひ來　　　　　　　　（杏々山莊）

花なりし日
師や愛でましし
椿の實
手にそと撫でて
山莊下<small>くだ</small>る

May Yen Ting

The *Chō-On* Society's 13th National *Tanka* Festival

oh dear teacher
please awake once again!
I have come here
to this great gathering
as your follower   (before her grave at the Tokeiji temple)

I will seek
the shadow of my teacher—
in my mind
when I go back to her mountain villa,
the faint scent of incense   *(Yō-Yō Mountain Villa)*

how my teacher loved
the camellias in bloom—
stroking the flowers gently
I descend the path
from her mountain villa

この道を
究めん社友の
意氣堂に
籠りて 行 の
座にある如し　　　　　　（奥湯河原會場）

名指されて
出來惡き生徒の
とまどひに
立ちたり五百
社友の眞中

海波なる
大國の北京
詣でにぞ
憂ひ連なる
我等が行方　　　　　　　（大會詠草）

eager to master
the Way of tanka, *my colleagues*
in the society
seclude themselves in the hall
behaving like religious ascetics   (at Okuyugawara Hall)

my name was called
and I stood up, embarrassed
like a pupil with a poor record,
amid 500 colleagues
from the tanka *society*

in the wake of great waves
making their pilgrimages
to the big nation's Beijing,
come grave concerns
for the future of us all   (my tanka contributed to the National Festival)

北陸行

夏瘦せの
岩肌あらはに
溝深し
富士口開けて
我が機下にあり

懐ひ來て
久し北陸
日本海
廻れる機首の
眞下に蒼し

兼六園
一木一草に
佇みて
百萬石の
跡を尋むる

May Yen Ting

Going to the Hokuriku Area of Japan

below my aircraft,
its rocks laid bare
in summer,
yawns the deep-gulfed
crater of Mt. Fuji

I have been longing
for this trip to the Hokuriku —
right below my aircraft
flying over the Japan sea,
is the familiar indigo blue

I linger at each tree,
every plant
in Kenrokuen Gardens,
tracing the old history
of the prosperous era

降る雨に
いよよ日本の
姿なる
金茶寮庭の
<ruby>きんちやれう</ruby>
白砂青松

永平寺
七堂伽藍
巡りつつ
縁なき衆生
我が身の負ひ目

一塊の
陶土老匠の
手のリズムに
伸び縮みして
器となり行く　　　　　　　（九谷焼）

102

through the falling rain
an image of Japan comes to me
more and more clearly:
the white sand and green pines
of the Kincharyō Garden

as I walk around
the seven halls of the Eiheiji temple
I feel burdened
by my lack of connection
to the Buddhist faithful

stretching and shrinking
to the rhythm
of the master potter's hands,
a lump of earth
is becoming a vessel   (Kutani ware)

米大陸曠野を行く

満目の
曠野枯草
一色を
直走る<ruby>車<rt>カー</rt></ruby>の
點綴の<ruby>彩<rt>いろ</rt></ruby>　　　　　　（西北諸州）

幾曲り
河に沿ひ來て
陽を反す
淀みに白帆
一つ淨きをり　　　　　　（コロンビア河）

<ruby>蛇<rt>スネーク</rt></ruby> 河
曠野三州
くねり來て
きらめきにつつ
コロンビア河に入る

104

May Yen Ting

Going to the American Continent's Open Plains

a line of colored cars
runs straight across
the monochrome dried grass
of prairies that stretch
as far as the eye can see   (the Northwestern states)

having followed
numerous bends in the river,
a single white sail
now floats in a pool
reflecting the sun   (the Columbia River)

the Snake River
winds around three states
in the prairies,
then sparkling and gleaming
pours into the Columbia River

假居

雑草取り
芝生に映る
蒲公英の
花の黄に手の
暫しためらふ

忍従の
幻影かとも
垣沿ひに
頭垂れ咲く
紫陽花の色

南天は白
紫陽花は青
庭に自が
孤恃みて
今を咲き闌く　　　　　（ふもと會詠草）

アメリカに
育ちし嫁が
奇異とせり
夫婦茶碗の
大小の別

May Yen Ting

Temporary Lodgings

I'm plucking weeds
from the lawn
and my hand lingers
on the shining yellow
of dandelion flowers

I wonder if this
is an illusion of submission—
along the fence line
the colors of hydrangea
in bloom hanging their heads

in the green garden
nandina and white hydrangeas
forming
their own arcs, now
in advanced bloom   (a tanka for the Fumoto society)

to my son's wife
raised in America,
it seems strange,
this distinction in size
between husband and wife tea cups

107

我が妻の
座を寡婦の友ら
待ちてをり
<small>フイールチエア</small>
車椅子におほらかに
物言ふ一人　　　　　　　（ミセステーラー）

統治者

民主々義の
國の逐鹿
幾月ぞ
互みに骨身
削られにつつ　　　　　（カーター氏らのキャンペーン）

八億に
飢させざると
功擧げて
大屠殺せし
過去世は問はず

my widowed friends
are waiting to take my seat
as a wife,
says someone in a wheel-chair
speaking frankly　　　　　　　(Mrs. Taylor)

The Ruler

how many months
do these contests last
in democracies,
while the opponents
tear strips off each other　　　　(Mr. Carter's campaign)

citing the merit
of eight hundred million
saved from starvation,
this world does not question
the past vast slaughter

瀬戸の海

昭六會卒業四十五周年紀念旅行

紅顔は
世と移ろへど
昭六會
今宵祝ぎ合ふ
互ひの健在

ピークオン
批孔の
　　はるけ
聲に杳く
しずたに
閑谷廟
かい
楷の紅葉を
前に鎮まる　　　　　　　　（池田藩閑谷學校孔子廟、楷＝孔樹）

黒き門
今に開きて
大石良雄
立ち出でますか
赤穂城長屋

May Yen Ting

The Seto Inland Sea

A trip to commemorate the 45th anniversary of the 1931 graduates of Hitotsubashi University.

although our rosy cheeks

have changed over time,

tonight we meet

to celebrate graduating in 1931

and each other's good health

far from the critical voice

of Confucius,

the Shizutani shrine

lies calm, with a kai *tree*

scarlet-leafed, at its front   *(Ikeda Clan Shizutani School Confucius Shrine)*

[Editor's Note: The *kai* tree is the Chinese pistache tree. It is also known as the Confucius tree whose seeds were brought from Confucius' grave site in Shandong, China and are often planted in Confucian temples.]

will Ōishi Yoshio

open the black gates

and emerge now?

I'm in front of the long house

of Akō castle

これよりは
俺らが國か
お猿木に
枝搖するなり
我ら見下して　　　　　　（小豆島お猿の國）

擦り寄りて
袖引きにつつ
我が顔を
仰ぐ猿の目
瞬きもせず

岩肌の
襞も細かに
織りなせり
紅葉錦の
寒霞渓谿

吉備津神社
銀杏落葉の
大前に
雙手合せし
無我のたまゆら

112

"this is our land, here,
isn't it?" —
a big monkey
swinging from a tree branch
looks down on us   (Shōdoshima Monkeyland)

snuggling up to me
and pulling at my sleeve,
the monkey gazes
unblinking
into my face

woven into
the narrow creases
of the rock's surface
is a brocade of scarlet leaves,
in the Kankakei valley

at the Kibitsu shrine
I put my hands together in prayer
to the gods present
there amid the fallen gingko leaves…
a short pause of selflessness

打たん手を
逃れ行きけり
ゴキブリは
夜の疊を
背な艶やかに　　　　　　　（下津井の宿）

學びの日
幾往復の
瀬戸の海
今日遙か來ぬ
今ひと度の逢ひ

波の音
モーターボートの音
響かひて
瀬戸内懐古の
夜は覺めがちに

cockroaches
scuttled away from the hand
about to strike,
their backs shining at night
on the tatami-mat floor   *(lodgings in Shimotsui)*

when I was studying
I made numerous return trips
across the Seto Sea—
today I've come from afar
to meet for one more time

the sound of the waves,
the sound of motorboats echoing—
I wake often
through the night
by this nostalgic Seto Sea

京の秋

我目ざし
飛鳥となりて
來る友を
しかと受止めぬ
京のプラットホーム　　　　（植松節子様）

て
掌ひろげて
ホームを一散に
我に來し
一人の友の
満面の笑み

身も心も
優しうなりぬ
京一夜
連峰の月
明け六つの鐘

水の青
底に沈めて
谿々の
紅葉時雨に
色勝り行く

May Yen Ting

The Capital in Autumn

along the platform
at Kyoto, aiming for me
like a bird on the wing,
comes my friend, caught now
firmly in my embrace   (Uematsu Setsuko-sama)

there she was
my friend dashing towards me
at full speed
with her arms outstretched, and
a big smile all over her face

body and mind grew gentler
one night in Kyoto
with the moon
over the mountain peak
and six peals of a dawn bell

the blue of the water
sinks to the river bottom,
and through the valleys
autumn leaves are coloring
more vividly after rain showers

たたなはる
山の狭間の
又奥の
紅葉も目路に
高山寺の縁

詩仙堂
白山茶花が
引き出でし
楓、柿の實、
千兩の色

at Kōzanji temple
from the veranda, I can see too
scarlet leaves spread
further into the ravines
between overlapping mountains

in the Shisendo garden
white sasanqua
accentuated
by the colors of maple trees,
persimmon fruit, and senryō *shrubs*

桂離宮

黄塵を
拂ひ透垣の
下に威儀
正すがに入りぬ
桂の離宮

こも
薦巻きに
寒を耐へ來て
幾世紀
桂離宮の
むら
一叢蘇鐵

名園の
折の紅葉を
よそに早や
冬籠り行く
薦巻き蘇鐵

May Yen Ting

Katsura Imperial Villa

brushing off yellow dust,
I assumed
a dignified sort of attitude
to go under the arbor lattice
into the Katsura Imperial Villa

wrapped in straw matting,
how many centuries
has it withstood the cold,
this clump of cycads
at the Katsura Imperial Villa?

though this famous garden
still has the scarlet leaves
of the season,
the cycads are already wrapped
in straw matting for winter

老人の日

市長より
茶碗四つ
受く我
正に高齢者かや
今日老人の日

恙なく
今日ありしかば
又明日を
恃まん餘生
確かに刻み

動物園
老人半額の
入場に
はしやぎて頓に
寂しくなりぬ

とよもして
自づと倒れたり
老木の
一瞬の終<ruby>終<rt>つひ</rt></ruby>よ
山に出で逢ふ

Elders' Day

today, Elders' Day,
I receive four tea bowls
from the mayor—
am I really now
an aged person?

today has passed
smoothly, and so
I will trust tomorrow, too,
with the certainty
of the rest of my life

over-excited
at the gate to the zoo
where seniors enter
for half price,
suddenly I feel lonely

the instant end of an old tree
which had crashed down
of its own accord—
I encounter this tree
out on the mountain

死を忌み
言ふ夫に背きて
小夜床に
己が最期を
思ひ巡らす

今<ruby>一生<rt>ひとよ</rt></ruby>
とは思はねど
たゆたへる
故國の行方
見極めんもの

述懐

逝きし子の
如く時には
憶ひをり
沒となりにし
初二十首詠

己が言
讓らざる聲
高まりて
ふと途切れたり
夫と子の對話

to my husband
who taboos talk of death,
I turn my back
and in the evening lie in bed
contemplating my last moments

it's not that
I'd like another life, but
I do want to probe
the future of the old country,
my fluctuating motherland

Reminiscences

as if it were
a dead child, sometimes
I'm remembering
my first batch of twenty tanka
turned down for publication

unwilling to yield
to the other's opinions,
their voices rose, then
suddenly broke off—dialogue
between my husband and our child

我が弟
街ひへつらひ
拙なくて
地質學にし
<ruby>一生<rt>ひとよ</rt></ruby>かくるか

父の左右
爭ひ寝ねし
幼な日の
弟らよ位牌
父に添ひ立つ

意地見すと
國連の籍
投げ棄てつ
今にして歴史の
悔となりぬる

my younger brother,
unskilled at flattery,
perhaps he will
devote his entire life
to the study of geology

oh, my younger brothers
in childhood squabbling
over which side of father they slept —
now their mortuary tablets
stand in line with his

displaying obstinacy
in casting off membership
of the United Nations:
this now has become
a regretful part of our history

冬日

天霧ひ
向つ山雨
降れるらし
冷え冷えと
顔を撲ちて来るもの

青芝を
圍ふ盛りの
萬壽菊
ま冬の庭に
金色<ruby>金色<rt>こんじき</rt></ruby>放つ

西東
權力者らの
顛落を
見守り次ぎつつ
年改まる

首相たる
前身の今日
裁かるる
自が感慨か
涙と<ruby>下<rt>くだ</rt></ruby>りぬ

Winter Days

in the mountains opposite
shrouded by mist,
it seems to be raining…
something chilly
is striking my face, too

encircling the green lawn
is an abundance of marigolds,
displaying
their golden tones
in the mid-winter garden

the year changes
while we keep on witnessing
the collapses
of Western and Eastern powers
one after the other

tried today in court
as former Prime Minister —
was it his
genuine deep emotion
that set his tears flowing?

1977

春

棚隅に
置き忘られし
水仙の
根の呼ぶ春や
か細き芽立ち

<ruby>飄<rt>へう</rt></ruby>々と
木々を撲ち行く
春あらし
空に金無垢
半月の<ruby>光<rt>かげ</rt></ruby>

春麗ら
洗濯物を
三竿程
干し上げて今日
しかと我在り

Spring

left and forgotten
in a corner of the shelves,
daffodil bulbs
growing slender sprouts
remind me it's spring

the roaring winds
of a fierce spring storm
beating the trees, and
in the sky, the gleam of
a pure gold half moon

beautiful spring weather:
hanging up the washing
to dry on three poles,
today for sure
I am alive

涙ひた落つ

福建省より數代前の祖渡來、基隆河上流に卜居

鮎に名を
獲し故里か
鯀魚坑
<ruby>けつぎょこう</ruby>
渡來の祖の
<ruby>おや</ruby>
卜せし川邊
<ruby>ぼく</ruby>

國喪の
<ruby>こくさう</ruby>
喪章の袖を
たくし上げ
我が川遊び
明治童女期

片言の
日本語の少女
國出でて
東都四賀師に
見えし 縁
<ruby>えにし</ruby>

May Yen Ting

A Torrent of Tears

From Fukien province, ancestors several generations back came to Taiwan and settled in the upper reaches of the Keelung River.

did the old village

take its name from the fish,

'ayu'?

my ancestors came from Ketsugyokō

to settle on the river banks

pushing up my sleeve

with its band

for national mourning,

I played by the river

in my Meiji girlhood

as a young girl

with only partial command of Japanese,

I left my country

and in Tokyo formed

a strong bond with teacher Shiga

垂乳根に
ま向ふ如く
み教へに
頷き聽きぬ
學び舍の日々

震災に
離散してより
五十年
面影胸に
抱き續けぬ

斷たれぬと
見し緣の絲
手繰られて
み手に再び
縋り得し幸

まづき子程
愛しく思ふ
垂乳根や
師の愛我は
獨り鍾めぬ

as if I were facing
my honorable mother,
I nodded my head
and heeded the teachings
of those high school days

since we were separated
by that natural disaster
fifty years ago,
I've continued to hold
her face in my heart

it seemed severed, to me,
but that string to the past
is tugged, and again
I entrust my happiness
to your kind hands

one was as dear to her,
this womanly woman,
as an awkward child —
a teacher's love
I alone collected

おほけなし
拙き身の名
み歌はた
今際^{いまは}の御書に
殘され賜びぬ

老いの眼の
所爲^{せい}にのみかは
逝きましし
師憶ひ出づれば
涙直^{ひた}落つ

才^{さい}はあらね
歌のみ跡を
ひたすらに
追はん命の
殘れる限り

I am so honored
that she deigned to record
my humble name
among the tanka
in her very last book

surely it's not just
because of my aged eyes
that whenever
I remember my deceased teacher
there comes a torrent of tears

though I have no talent
I will earnestly
pursue
only the tanka *path*
for the rest of my life

一周忌

遙けくも
天翔けり來まし
我が夢に
師はたち給ふ
優しく笑まひ

追悼號
讀み返しつつ
在りし日の
み姿を今に
四賀師一周忌

詮ぞなき
腰痛とふ記事
讀みてをり
四賀師いまはに
惱まされしこれ

四賀師への
書「先生」と
<ruby>書<rt>ふみ</rt></ruby>
書き出して
少女に返り
甘えたりしを

May Yen Ting

One Year Anniversary of the Death

I dreamed of flying over
from far away in the sky,
and my teacher
standing there
smiling tenderly

reading over and over
the commemorative issue of the journal,
I remember her as she was,
on this, the first anniversary
of my teacher, Ms. Shiga's death

I'm reading an article
that tells of the untreatable
hip pain she suffered —
oh, Ms. Shiga how agonizing
your final hours must have been

in the letter to Ms. Shiga
I addressed her as 'dear teacher'
in remembrance
of her fond indulgence
to me as a young girl

潮音社師友

調べ高く
太く詠ひて
逝かれしか
悲しく雄々し
信濃の古武士　　　　　　　　（峯村國一先生）

相擁して
哭かまほし師の
御影負ひ
遙か來ましし
一人の友　　　　　　　　　　（森満江様）

萬感は
言葉こ出でず
遙々と
來ましし友を
正面に抱く

May Yen Ting

Friends from the *Chō-On Tanka* Society

did he pass away
reciting melodically,
in a fulsome way?
he was a sorrowful, brave
old warrior from Shinano   (Minemura Kuniichi-sensei)

a friend came from afar,
carrying her own image
of our teacher—
to weep in each other's arms,
was what we wanted   (Mori Mitsue-sama)

ten thousand feelings
are not put into words—
I hold this friend,
who has come from afar,
in a full embrace

朝夕に

行く道に
四肢投げをる犬
我が遣りし
視線と合ひて
眸伏せたり

石段二百
樟の落實を
一つづつ
踏み鳴らし踏み
鳴らし息を整ふ

膝屈折
執念く雜草も
引き抜きぬ
庭芝の上の
朝の體操

ころころと
轉がる如し
巣立ち鳥
我が前抜けて
木の下闇に

Morning and Evening

on the path I walk
was a dog
flinging about its limbs —
meeting my gaze
it closed its eyes

on the two hundred steps
of the stone staircase
I keep treading
on fallen acorns, crunch, crunch,
as I breathe steadily

bending and flexing my knees,
tenaciously
I weeded the garden:
my morning exercise
on the lawn

tumbling over and over
young birds
leaving their nest
pass through my vision
in the darkness under the trees

屋根越えて
温泉宿の流し
木曽節を
先に今宵は
日本の調べ

主婦逝きし
隣家の父子
忙しげに
物炒めをり
鐵鍋の音

一堂に
寄りて嫡庶子
タブーの如く
父を語らず
その四十周忌

from over the rooftops
flowing into the hot spring inn
wandering minstrel songs
I hear first tonight
the melodies of Japan

in the neighboring house
where the wife has died,
father and child
bustle about cooking
with a clatter of pans

together under one roof,
legitimate and illegitimate children—
as if tabooed,
they avoid talking of their father
on the fortieth anniversary of his death

米國の日々

老なりの
氣力振ひて
裏藪の
枯木樵りをり
異國に假り住み

おふくろの
味と寄り來し
子孫らに_{うまご}
唐人街の豆腐に_{チャイナタウン}
京の柚味噌

人歩まぬ
歩道をい行く
紛れなき
異邦人我の
小さき孤影

裏立木を
透り來し陽に
芝草の
發つる碧は_{みどり}
色華やかに

May Yen Ting

My Time in America

swinging with the vigor
of an elderly person,
I'm cutting down
dead trees in the rear thicket —
living at leisure in a foreign land

for my grandchildren
who've come to rely on the taste
of 'Mom's home cooking,'
I add tofu from Chinatown
and yuzu miso paste from Kyoto

going onto the footpath
where no one walks,
I am unmistakable
as a strange foreigner
with my small, solitary shadow

in the sunshine
filtering through the trees
at the back
green color springs from the lawns
gleaming brilliantly

届かざる
裏の高木の
櫻桃を
朝夕仰ぎて
色愛でてをり

一本の
チェリー界隈の
鳥集め
さざめく聲に
實零るる音

高木より
鳥の時々
落せしチェリー
拾ひ食うべて
うま味確めし

たをやかに
咲き靡く
我がミニ畑の
萩に通ふ如し
午_{ひる}の白蝶

morning and evening
I look up at the cherries
on high branches
beyond my reach,
admiring their color

in a single cherry tree
the neighborhood birds are gathered,
twittering—
amid their voices I hear
the sound of fruit dropping

picking up and eating
cherries dropped occasionally
by the birds
in the tall trees,
I confirmed their sweetness

in the daytime white butterflies
seem to commute around
my mini-field
to the bush-clover whose flowers
flutter elegantly in bloom

束の間の
花の開きと
知りつつも
手折り來たりぬ
野牡丹の紫

荒草を
抜き出でし黄の
光彩よ
野に置くに惜し
金ぽうげの花

散歩道
盡きて仄かに
匂ひ來る
花の在り處は
知らざるままに

枝の張り
收めて一樹
やんはりと
眠りに入りぬ
夜闇の合歓の木

though realizing
this flower will be open
only briefly,
I've picked a wild peony,
a purple one

oh, those bright yellow gleams
poking out from wild grasses...
it seems a shame
to leave the buttercups
there in the field

coming to the end
of the walking trail
I smell a faint fragrance,
not knowing where
there are flowers growing

stretching its branches
as far as it could,
the tree
has gone quietly to sleep:
a silk tree in night darkness

移り來て
樵りし庭木の
小枝らの
芥となれる
ひそかな月日

夏の日に
播きし菜の歯に
やや強し
食みつつ歸る
日を思ひをり

見知らぬを
行き逢へば先づ
beautiful day と
讃へかけ來る
米人の朝

思ひきや
五十餘年の
時返し
米大陸に
師に見えんとは　　　　　　（遠山 [松岡] 千代子先生）

the small branches
from the garden trees
I cut down
after moving here, over time
will quietly become waste

chewing hard
at the tough mustard greens
planted in summer,
I am considering
the day for my return

when I encounter
on the path in the morning
an unknown American,
he first praises the weather
saying, "it's a beautiful day"

it has been
more than fifty years!
I never thought
to see that teacher
in America again   *(Toyama [Matsuoka] Chiyoko-sensei)*

男めき
初めにし孫に
ま對ひて
氣壓されるつつ
眩しみ見るも

名を分けし
新孫梅玲の
生ひ先の
我在らぬ世を
ふと描き見ぬ

事もなき
日々にしあれど
ふと胸を
衝き來るは危惧か
物佗しさか

歌作り
行の如くに
ひたすらに
己れ勵ます
殘りの命

confronted with
a grandson who has begun
to look like a man,
I'm too overcome and dazzled
to take him all in

I share my name
with my new granddaughter, Mayleen —
the part of the world
where she is growing up without me,
suddenly swims before my eyes

though there's nothing
of special concern these days,
something suddenly
prods my heart — is it
misgiving or lonesomeness?

I compose tanka
as if carrying out
a religious practice,
earnestly encouraging myself
to do so for the rest of my life

閉ぢて行く
家の落葉を
掃き掃きて
暫し心の
安らぎにをり

空港に
急ぐ峽路の
いち早き
紅葉の色に
心殘し來つ

太平洋
行きつ戻りつ
年經りぬ
何處や我の
終の地ならん

<ruby>有體<rt>ありてい</rt></ruby>は
日和見主義か
國二つ
股かけ住める
己が疚しさ

sweeping, sweeping
fallen leaves from the house
I'm going to close up,
for a while I am
soothing myself

I hurried to the airport,
leaving my heart behind
amid the colors
of early autumn leaves
on the valley paths

years have passed
as I go and come
across the Pacific—
I wonder where
my final resting place will be

put bluntly,
is this 'sitting on the fence'?
I feel guilty
picking and choosing
between two countries to live in

東都に寄る

立ち寄りし
東都人波に
揉まれつつ
我も日本人の
顔になりをり

逝きし友
行方知らぬ友
病める友
全部話に
のせてクラス會　　　　　　　（お茶の水女子學文科）

クラス會
半世紀經て
懇ろに
教へあふなり
自が治病體驗

May Yen Ting

Dropping in to Tokyo

dropping in to Tokyo
I'm buffeted
by waves of people—
I too am getting to have
a Japanese face

friends who've passed away
friends whose whereabouts are unknown,
ailing friends—
we touch on the subject
of all of them, at the class reunion   (of the Literature Department of Ochanomizu
                                           Women's University)

meeting at the class reunion
after half a century,
we tell each other in detail
about our respective experiences
of recovery from illnesses

歸り來たる

椅子に乘り
枝傾けて
確めぬ
枇杷の小花の
初咲きの色

點綴する
如く葉の上に
二つ三つ
顯ち並べたり
山茶花の紅

仰ぎ見る
校舎の屋根に
根づきるし
芒の穗群
小止みなく搖る

同郷の
老人會を
逃げてるし
夫はいつしか
常連となり

Back Home

standing on a chair,
I bent over a branch
to check the color
of the first little blooms
on the loquat tree

like scattered dots
the scarlet colors
of two or three
sasanqua camellias
have appeared on the leaves

looking up
I see rooted
on the college roof
pampas grasses
ceaselessly swaying

my husband,
who used to avoid meetings
of the aged in our village,
without noticing,
has become a regular member

東京より友來訪

友二人
彌次喜多と老い
覺束なに
我を訪ひ來ぬ
臺灣初旅　　　　　　　　（東京府立一高女級友）

會ひをれば
我ら少女と
はしやぐなり
互ひの耄碌
肴にしつつ

May Yen Ting

Friends Come to Visit from Tokyo

two elderly friends

on their first trip in Taiwan

came to visit me,

as awkward and unconfident

as the comic characters, Yaji and Kita   (classmates from Tokyo Prefectural First
                                                  Girls' High School)

when we meet

we frolic like young girls,

chatting

about trivialities

in our second childhood

1978

古掛け時計

捨てかねし
古掛け時計に
リズム合せ
閑職の夫と
我の明けくれ

こだはり來し
腺腫を切ると
夫は言ふ
肯ひにつつ
懼れつつ聞く

推床 に
_{おしベッド}
笑顔一つを
乗せて夫
手術室より
推され出で來ぬ

脚下の
町闇に潜めど
空の彩
先づ高樓に
元旦生れぬ

May Yen Ting

The Old Wall Clock

to the rhythm
of the old pendulum clock
we couldn't abandon,
my leisured husband and I
pass our days and nights

the swollen glands
that have been of concern
for some time,
he'll have removed, says my husband—
hearing this, I agree fearfully

lying there
with a smiling face
my husband came out
of the operating theater,
propelled on a hospital trolley

while the town at my feet
was hidden in the darkness,
the colors of the sky
gave birth to New Year's morning
first over the tall buildings

十一階
術後のベッドの
夫に告ぐ
ま向ふ屋根の
大き初日を

幾葉の
訃報賀狀に
混り來ぬ
逝く年來る年
いやしみじみと

庭櫻
よく見ゆる位置に
椅子置きて
術後の夫に
我がする理髮

May Yen Ting

I tell my husband,
in bed on the 11th floor
after his operation,
of the great New Year's sunrise
on the roof directly opposite

several death notifications
arrived among the New Year cards —
I'm keenly aware
of the year that has passed
and the year to come

I place a chair
where he can get a good view
of our garden's cherry blossoms,
then give my husband
a post-operative hair cut

よろばへる
歩み見せつつ
口のみの
夫の強がり
響く芝生に

じわじわと
身<ruby>内<rt>みうち</rt></ruby>を蝕む
ものやある
ま夜に覺めては
耳澄し聞く

憾みなき
<ruby>終<rt>つひ</rt></ruby>を願へば
埒あかぬ
課題の如く
胸にもたるる

I watch him
staggering to walk,
it is only
his bluffing talk
that resounds on the lawn

there is something
gradually eating up
my body—
waking in the middle of the night
I hear it with clear ears

if I wish
for an end without regrets,
it seems
to incline my mind
toward insoluble issues

春色

枇杷の實は
圓らに著し
降る雨に
金の産毛の
水彈きつつ

拓かれし
尾根に月桃の
一叢よ
春の嵐に
はためき止まぬ

元旦の
めでたさ呼ぶや
隣り家の
我が家のなべて
緋櫻の色　　　　　　　　（舊暦正月）

174

May Yen Ting

Spring Hues

the loquat fruits
are remarkably round—
in the falling rain
water bounces
off their golden down

on the mountain ridge,
in a clearing, clumped together,
getto plants—
they flutter ceaselessly
in the spring storms

welcoming
felicitations on New Year's Day—
at the neighbor's house
and our house, everywhere
the crimson color of cherry blossoms (The Lunar New Year)

175

兩雄の死

幾多の血
流して中華を
奪り合ひしか
兩雄壽盡き
歷史新たに

あちら宥め
こちらすかして
中東へ
和平と武器を
併せ賣り込む

熱き戀
法に觸れしと
サウド王女
擊たれ曝さる
沙漠の土に

May Yen Ting

The Deaths of Two Heroes

how much blood was spilt
as they fought each other
for control of China?
the two heroes' luck now exhausted,
a new page in history is turned

soothing there,
flattering here,
in tandem they sell
peace and military weapons
to the Middle East

a Saudi Princess
whose passionate love
contravened the law,
shot and left exposed
in the desert

級友來臺

お茶の女子大學文科

遙けくも
相扶けつつ
友ら來ぬ
此處に卒業
五十年祝ぐべく

世移ろひ
國異なりて
幾十年
變らぬ友情
溫め來つる

娘<ruby>娘<rt>こ</rt></ruby>のお骨
<ruby>湖<rt>うみ</rt></ruby>に鎭めん
友に添ふ
日月潭の
明けの棧橋

May Yen Ting

Classmates Come to Taiwan

Classmates from the Literature Department of Ochanomizu Women's University.

from a great distance,
supporting each other,
friends came here
needing to celebrate the fifty years
since we graduated

the world moves on
and our countries are different,
but we have kept
the warmth of our friendship
unchanged over decades

her daughter's bones
will come to rest in its depths —
I accompany my friend
at dawn, to the wharf
of the Sun Moon Lake

春三月

仰ぐ目に
安らに見ゆる
天明の
月に寄り添ふ
星影一つ

初蛙
抜け駆け來しか
裏口に
季(とき)まだき聲
高々と揚ぐ

庭に向け
据ゑし机に
櫻(はな)眺め
若葉めでつつ
歌思ふ日々

自が得體(えたい)
時に自問す
障子ある
家に起き臥し
歌作三昧

May Yen Ting

March, Spring

in my upward gaze
peacefully appears
the shadow of one star
nestling beside the bright moon
in the heavens

have the first frogs
stolen a march on us?
at the back door
before morning breaks
their voices louder and louder

at the desk
placed to face the garden,
I spend days thinking of tanka
while I gaze at the cherry blossoms
and admire the young leaves

at times I question
my own nature—
living in a house
with sliding paper doors,
I compose tanka *absorbedly*

故里の家

親族家族
<small>うからやから</small>

犇き住める

日よ杳し

舊家失語の

義兄と幽かに
<small>あに</small>

百餘年

古き構への

稱揚さるや
<small>はや</small>

故里の廢屋

觀客を呼ぶ

May Yen Ting

My Home in the Old Village

oh, those days when
kith and kin lived cheek by jowl—
the dim sight of my brother-in-law
who has lost the power of speech,
and this dark old house he lives in

old construction styles
of a hundred or more years ago
are much admired—
the abandoned houses here
in my old village, draw sightseers

一人の友

五十年の
ひた心もて
會ひに來る
一人の友を
待つ春そぞろ

五十年の
思ひ語らず
人中に
かい添ひ行けば
心足らふらし

海越えて
み傍へに花
赤々と
咲き掲げよや
サルビア小粒の實　　　　（庭のサルビアの種を贈る）

May Yen Ting

One Friend

this spring enthusiasm
waiting for a friend to come
to our gathering,
a friend I've held in my heart
these fifty years

our thoughts unspoken
for fifty years, we walk
close together
through the crowds,
and our hearts are full

when you cross the sea
make your flowers
bloom bright red
beside her, oh little seeds
of salvia!   *(I will send her some salvia seeds from my garden)*

初蟬の聲

向山
包める木々の
さ緑を
深めて今日も
雨降り續く

曇り日の
木蔭に白き
しやがの花
蝶舞ひ縫ひて
ほしいままなる

突と揚り
忽ち止みし
初蟬は
ザボン一樹の
輝く邊り

May Yen Ting

Voices of the First Cicadas

deep into the green
of the trees enfolded
in the mountain beyond
today too rain
continues to fall

on a cloudy day
under the shade of the trees
butterflies
dance and weave at will
among white shaga *irises*

a sudden shrilling
that abruptly stopped —
the first cicadas
are in the vicinity
of a shining shaddock tree

記憶喪失の友

喪ひし
記憶呼ばんか
ベッドの上に
友の手撫でつ
頬擦り見つ
<small>さす</small>

我は誰
面寄せ行けば
たどたどと
友指書きぬ
丁とふ字らし

共防の約

共防の
約さりながら
小捨てて
大に就く世ぞ
昔も今も

（臺灣米國間共同防禦條約）

My Friend Suffering from Amnesia

will I call up
the memories she has lost?
I tried stroking the hands,
caressing the cheeks, of my friend
as she lay in bed

"who am I?"
I asked, going closer to her face—
falteringly
my friend wrote with her finger
something like the kanji, 'tei'

A Contract for Mutual Defense

a contract for mutual defense—
nonetheless, this is a world
where the small are abandoned
and they stick by the great—
so it was of old, so it is now   (the Taiwan USA Mutual Defense Treaty)

長弟病む

追ひ撃ちの
如く癌病む
弟に
腦血栓來ぬ
餘命幾何

このままに
果つる命か
ほほゑめば
白し艷もつ
弟の歯並み

弟よ
氣長に病ひ
癒せかし
父母の靈坐す
ここ齋明寺

我が負へば
足地に着くと
亡母言ひぬ
二つ下なる
弟の守り

190

May Yen Ting

My Oldest Younger Brother

it's like kicking a man
when he's down —
my brother with cancer
now has a brain thrombosis —
how much longer can he live?

is this
how his life will end?
when he smiles
I see the white gleam
of my brother's teeth

oh my brother,
may you take the time
to heal your ailments
here at the Saimyōji, where
the spirits of our parents dwell

my deceased mother told me
to take care of my brother,
two years younger —
carried on my back
his feet reached the ground

夏たけなはに

たけなはの
夏の暑さを
せり上げて
一谷に湧く
蟬の高聲

技を撓め
咲きたけ行けば
まん圓<ruby>き（まろ）
朱<ruby>（あけ）の花火か
繡毬とふ花

幾本の
高木の家居や
冴々と
鳥ら來鳴きて
思ふままなる

May Yen Ting

In Midsummer

vying with the heat
of summer in full swing,
the loud voices
of cicadas
swell through the valley

bending the branch
as it rises high and swells
into bloom, is it
a round red firecracker?
no, a viburnum flower

oh that house
with several tall trees —
at will
birds come singing
their pure clear songs

アメリカにて

長留守を
經て來て今年の
出で逢ひよ
眞夏に盛る
庭の紫陽花

胸張りて
立てる兵士の
横列に
隣家を限る
いぶき二十本

老いの力
振ひて木樵る
汗ばみを
ねぎらふ如し
吹き入る涼風

挑むがに
異國に庭の
枯木樵り
薪一山と
せし己が意地

May Yen Ting

In the United States

arriving back
after a long absence
for this year's encounter
with the hydrangeas
in our lush midsummer garden

chests puffed out,
standing like a row of soldiers,
twenty ibuki *trees*
draw the line between ours
and the neighbor's house

swinging at it
with my elderly strength
I cut the wood—
as if rewarding my pains,
a cool breeze gets up

as a kind of challenge
I'm chopping down
withered trees in a foreign garden,
my intention to make
a mountain of firewood

後世會はば
父母に告げまし
根限り
賜びし命を
我が生きたりと

何話す
事のなければ
今日かくて
在る幸夫と
繰り返し言ふ

氣負ふまじ
己が凡愚に
居坐りて
歌作りなば
樂しからまし

洗腦を
懼れ他國の
軒借りて
生き繼がんとや
齢古稀を過ぎ

if we meet in the next world
I want to tell my parents
that I have lived
the life they gave me
with all my might and main

even if there's nothing
to talk about,
we are lucky
to be here today, like this,
my husband and I repeat

mustn't be too eager —
if I just sit here
in my ordinary way
and compose tanka,
it should be fun

fearful of brain-washing,
shall I rent temporarily
in the other country
and go on living there
in celebration of my seventy years?

我に似て
丘にエトランゼの
影曳くか
夕陽を浴ぶる
公孫樹ひと本

瞠る目に
眩ゆき丘の
家一つ
入り陽集めて
黄金の造り

夢みるし
四つ葉のクローバよ
野に摘みて
幾日乙女の
心彈める

does this 'stranger'
on the hill trail a shadow
like me?
a single gingko is bathed
in the evening sunlight

I stare in wonder
at the dazzling hill-top house —
gathering in the rays
of the sinking sun,
it seems to be made of gold

oh, that four-leaf clover
I dreamed of finding —
when I picked one
in a field, my maiden heart was
pounding with excitement for days

キャンプデービッド會談

年かけて
談じ訴ふれど
和平なほ
遠し中東
宿怨の國

カーター氏
あの手この手に
兩頭を
駆せしかキャンプ
デービッド會談

握手して
肩を抱きぬ
相仇
ホワイトハウス
白　宮　に
中東和平へのショウ

May Yen Ting

The Camp David Talks

though they've had recourse
to discussions for many years now,
peace seems still far off
for countries in the Middle East
which harbor old grudges

at the Camp David talks
did Mr. Carter perhaps
perform a juggling act,
manipulating both
of the Heads of State?

shaking hands, hugging,
mutual enemies
at the White House
put on a show
of Middle Eastern peace

ニューポープ

あへなくも
ひそと逝きしか
ニューポープ
驚き収りて
哀惜切に

歸郷

歸り來て
心ゆるびぬ
木犀の
花故里の
香りに咲き闌く

何を又
見え分かぬ先に
戦(そよ)ぎをり
故里は
空蒼く花赤し

The New Pope

how was it the new Pope

passed away so unexpectedly,

almost in secret?

overcoming my surprise

I grieve wholeheartedly

Going Home

when I came back home

my heart was at ease —

osmanthus flowers

were in full bloom

with the fragrance of my birthplace

before I could tell

what they were, I saw

red flowers

trembling against the blue sky

of my home town

弟死す

物言はば
空しかるべし
目を瞑り
喘ぐ弟の
手握りやりぬ

病み次げる
<ruby>弟妹<rt>はらから</rt></ruby>思ふ
夜の更けて
突と起ちたり
<ruby>疾風<rt>はやて</rt></ruby>鳴る音

弟逝き
姪次ぎ逝きて
<ruby>義兄<rt>あに</rt></ruby>病みぬ
攻め立て來をる
目に見えぬもの

出土せし
お骨遺品に
<ruby>像<rt>イメージ</rt></ruby> 描けば
一世紀昔の
曽祖母近し

May Yen Ting

My Younger Brother Dies

whatever I say
would be empty words—
I grasped the hand
of my younger brother
who was gasping, eyes closed

I think of my younger brother
and my younger sister,
falling ill in succession—
deep in the night suddenly
fierce sounds of a gale

my younger brother died,
next my niece passed away,
then my brother-in-law fell ill—
something invisible
is coming to attack us

when I draw images
of unearthed bones
and other relics, I feel close
to my great-grandmother
of a century ago

平穏無事

朝づきて
目覺め咲くらし
溝際に
一叢白き
名の知らぬ花

幸せは
かく他愛なし
幾竿の
物干して湧く
この満ち足らひ

心關はる

過ぎ行きの
被統治民の
下意識
今も尾を曳き
我を卑屈にす

Safe and Sound

when morning comes
they seem to awake
and bloom —
these unknown white flowers
in a clump beside the drain

my happiness, so silly:
a sense of satisfaction
that wells up
when I've hung out to dry
several lines of washing

Concerning the Heart

the subconscious efforts
of past colonization
even today
are dragging on
making me servile

逃亡に
命冥加よ
顔弛め
ベトナム民ら
ドイツの地を踏む 　　　（テレビ畫面）

千餘萬
我らが行方を
頭越しに
規定せんとや
人權言ふ國

屠られて
人ら今亡し
平反の
諭天安門に
空しく響く

十億の
民の屏息
極りて
噴き上ぐらんか
固唾をぞ呑む

208

providential protection
for their escape!
with slackened faces
Vietnamese
tread the soil of Germany   *(on the TV screen)*

this country which
talks of human rights, is
about to determine the direction
of more than ten million of us,
over our heads and without consultation

the slaughtered people
are gone now —
around Tien An Men square, the sounds
of their exhortations for redress
reverberate, hollowly

will the hundred million
who have been cowed into silence,
finally rise up?
I am watching
with intense anxiety

斷交宣言

小人吹く
魔笛にカーター氏
現^{うつつ}なや
朋踏みにじり
踊り行きたり

堂々と
大統領の
名揭げて
夜驅け來りぬ
斷交宣言

賣られたる
民らの悲憤
血と噴きて
天を染めんか
師走の衢^{ちまた}

May Yen Ting

Announcement of a Disruption in Diplomatic Relations

has Mr. Carter gone mad
to the magic flute
played by a dwarf?
he tramples on his friends,
and goes dancing away

regally, under the banner
of the president's name,
in the night came
a hurried announcement
of a rupture in relations

will the resentment
of a sold-out people
erupt in blood, and
dye the sky above the streets
this December?

我が運命（さだめ）
かく権数家
幾人の
手に成り行くぞ
正しく見たる

民國よ
辛酸苦闘
堪へ堪へて
六十四餘年
歴史の歩み

街に湧く
聲識るや否
隣り家の
米少女庭に
犬と戯る

止め度なき
涙拭ひて
空見れば
枝頭に幾輪
緋櫻の色

my fate will thus
be lying in the hands
of however many
powerful politicians,
I saw that clearly

oh, the Republic of China!
it has endured, is still enduring
harshness and bitter struggles
throughout the progression
of more than sixty-four years history

is she not aware of the voices
welling up in the streets?
a young American girl
plays with her dog in the garden
of a neighboring house

wiping away my endless tears
I look at the sky —
on the top branches
are several bunches
of crimson cherry blossoms

カードゲーム

むざむざと
臺灣を抜き
捨て果てつ
大國が弄ぶ
カードゲームは

近代化の
助力を求め
自が謳ふ
反覇の路線
賣りつけんとす

昨日の是
今日非となりしか
走資派が
日米の尾追ふ
その國造り

正目もて
榮枯盛衰の
史實見つ
王中の王
パーレビの退去

The Card Game

the great powers
who have ended up
throwing out Taiwan
so readily
are playing a card game

asking for assistance
to modernize,
he is trying to sell
the anti-hegemony line
which he himself professes

has yesterday's positive
become today's negative?
the capitalist roaders chase
the tails of Japan and USA
for their national construction

with unblinking gaze
he witnessed
the prosperity and decline
that is history, then
King of Kings, Pahlavi, departed

駆られ來し
兵か前線に
うら若き
見目清らかに
クローズアップに映る　　（中越國境ベトナム兵）

are these soldiers

part of the forward advance?

close-up pictures

of very young men,

innocent in appearance   (soldiers at the border of China and Vietnam)

May Yen Ting

1979

219

早春

早春の
空靄こめて
緋櫻の
群咲く方の
ほのかな明り

裸木の
木百合の蕾
いち早し
赤子の空^{くう}に
振れる拳に

春空に
捧ぐる如し
たかだかと
百合の木一本
鴇^{とき}の花色

捨つるもの
捨て果て丘の
樟高木
陽にさみどりの
色反しつつ

Early Spring

early spring:
the faint light where
a clump of cherry trees
is in crimson bloom,
swirled with mist

on the bare African tulip tree
already there are
early buds
shaking their fists
at the sky, like babies

as if making offerings
to the spring sky,
the tulip tree
thrusts high its flowers
the color of ibis

finally discarding
all that is unnecessary,
the tall camphor trees
on the hill in the sun
reflecting pale green

ザボンの香
丘行く道を
漂へば
心おのづと
靜かに激ち來

獨り居を
隣家の知らぬ
飼鳥の
鋭き聲に
かかづらひをり

ビル街の
庭一枚の
ひら
芝の青
餘生の贅と
我が日々愛づる

曇り日の
闌けて幽かに
匂ひ來る
木蔭のしやがの
花よりならし

the fragrance of shaddock
floats around the path
to the hill —
of its own accord, my heart
becomes quietly excited

living alone,
I feel uneasy
about the shrill cries
of an unknown bird
kept by my neighbor

thinking of it
as luxury for the rest of my life,
everyday I enjoy
the garden's slice of green lawn
in a street of concrete buildings

the faint fragrance
on this cloudy day
must come from the shaga iris
in full bloom
beneath the trees' shade

在りし日に
包み申しし
み手の冷え
掌_{てのひら} にあり
今日三周忌　　　　　　（四賀師）

向山
なだれの緑
生ひ伸びて
廟は鴟尾の
み彩_{いろ}かすかなる

過去戀はず
未來思はず
庭芝に
雜草ひた拔く
安らぎ暫し

遺書かとも
友らに稀な
書_{ふみ}縷々と
書き次ぎあれば
春ぞ老_たけたる

the chill of those dear hands
I once wrapped with mine
lingers on my palms…
today is the third anniversary
of her passing   (my teacher, Shiga-sensei)

on the mountain opposite
an avalanche of green
is advancing—
on the shrine only the gargoyles
are faintly colored

neither nostalgic for the past,
nor contemplating the future,
for a while I enjoy
the calming effect of
earnestly weeding my lawn

are these my last words?
I keep on with detailed letters
for friends
to whom I rarely write,
while spring is coming to an end

恐懼

目覺め來て
まだ動悸あり
術もなく
追はれ追はれるし
斷崖の夢

あな空し
讀まず放てり
我 與_{あづか}らぬ
二十一世紀
展望の記事

月毎に
命確かめ
身の不調
宥めあふ我ら
老いらくの會ひ　　　　　（同學月例會）

散歩道
盡くれば戻りつつ
ふと思ふ
何時かい行きて
戻りなき道

226

May Yen Ting

Fear and Dread

awake now, but
my heart is still throbbing—
a dream of being helpless
as I'm chased
over a precipice

I let go of
such useless stuff
without reading it—
not my concern, that article
on the outlook for century 21

meeting every month,
we oldies
check we're alive
and console each other
about our bodily disorders   *(monthly classmates' meetings)*

come to the end
of the trail, I turn back
suddenly wondering
when I shall take a path
from which there is no return

お骨も墓も
いらぬと言はば
天邪鬼か
思ひ來て今
切なる願ひ

振り向けば
藥煎る背に
手合せるし
その夫語る
友聲を呑む

待たるるか
如水會より
喜壽の杖
老いは足からと
夫頻りに言ふ

萱草に
纏ひて咲ける
野朝顔の
色冴え冴えと
朝目に涼し

when I declare
I don't want bones or a grave,
I wonder whether
that's perverse, then pray
for my wish, earnestly

my friend choked up
telling me she turned round
to find her husband,
for whom she was infusing herbs,
with his hands together on her back

is he waiting for a cane
from the Josuikai *as a gift*
for his seventy-seventh birthday?
my husband frequently says
old age starts at the legs

the color of daylilies
blooming, wrapped round the reeds
looks so bright,
so clear and fresh,
in my morning eyes

義兄入院

病む義兄の
頻りに咳く聲
族皆
散りし古家に
響き渡らふ

歸り來ん
日やある入院の
兄連れて
空の古家を
しかと閉てたり

刻を待つ
義兄の命か
見守る目を
放てば外の面は
梅雨空低し

My Oldest Brother-in-Law is Hospitalized

the coughing
of my sick oldest brother-in-law
echoes loudly
through the old house now
his family is all scattered

someday he might be able
to return home — taking my brother
for hospital admission,
I closed the door tightly
on his empty old house

is my brother's life
ticking away?
when I take my eyes off him,
I see outside the low sky
of the rainy season

渡米の途に

初踏みし
成田空港
闘争の
跡にや芝の
色目にやさし

鎮りて
みどり被ける
山荘の
内外（うちそと）に師の
御影目に尋（と）む　　　　　　　（杳々山荘）

みうつしゑに
ま向へば
面傾けて
我に優しく
笑まひを賜ふ

草を抜き
み墓を清め
参らせて
師と暫し在る
心の安らぎ　　　　　　　　　（東慶寺）

May Yen Ting

On the Way Over to America

the first time
I entered Narita airport
was in the aftermath of conflict—
the color of the turf
was soft to my eyes

the shadow of my teacher
begs my gaze
both inside and outside
the mountain villa
peacefully clad in green   (Yō-Yō Mountain Villa)

when I look
straight into her picture,
face tilted
she is smiling gently
and kindly, at me

I go to her grave
to pull out the weeds and clean it—
for the short while
I'm with my teacher
my heart is soothed   (the Tokeiji temple)

漂流の
難民となる番ぞ
テレビが
日々冒頭に
告ぐるスローガン　　　（ふもと會詠草）

亡命の如く

重ね來し
身内らの死の
幻影を
絶つがに國を
翔び立ちて來ぬ

釋かん術
なき危惧一つ
亡命の
如くアメリカに
來てひそと住む

異國に來て
蟄居の節目か
手紙書き
新聞讀みて
テレビニュースを待つ

is it our turn
to become 'boat people'?
every day
on the TV headlines
this expression appears   (tanka *from the Fumoto* Tanka *Society)*

Like Losing One's Life

it's as if I've flown away
from my country, and come here
to extinguish
the illusion of deaths
multiplying in my family

with a misgiving
I've no way to explain,
I arrive in America
to live quietly
like someone seeking asylum

I've come to a foreign land;
is this my turning point
for staying indoors?
I write letters, read newspapers,
wait for the TV news

些かの
庭に故國の
菜の種を
播きて生長
待ち佗ぶる日々

挑むがに
老い意地張る
がに一枚の
芝丹念に
剪刀もて刈る

草刈や
隣家 mower の
轟音に
我が手の剪刀
音冴えもせず

夕されば
さ庭に來ては
幼な聲
あげつつ遊ぶ
懸巣の幾つ

May Yen Ting

I sow the seeds of greens
from the old country
in my tiny garden here
waiting for them to grow
day after wretched day

as if to challenge myself
as if to test
my stubborn old will,
I carefully cut with shears
a section of the lawn

cutting the grass
to the throbbing of the mower
at my neighbor's house,
the sound of my hand shears
is almost inaudible

when evening is nigh,
into my little garden
come a number of jays
raising their young voices
playfully

櫻の木を
目あてに訪ひ行く
エリックソン家
家毎の木々を
目に追ひながら　　　　　　（エリックソン紀美様）

空青く
曠野みどりに
家白し
幼なが描くに
似る車窓の景　　　　　　　（オレゴン州中部）

老いの目に
眩しみ仰ぐも
ボーイフレンド
連れて訪ひ來し
混血の孫

亡くなつたか
口衝き出でつ
カンカンの
死物々しかり
TV の畫面に　　　　　　　（米國 NBC TV）

May Yen Ting

I go to visit
the Ericksons, with the aim
of viewing their cherry trees,
on the way there looking
at the trees of all the homes   (Mrs. Kimi Erickson)

with its blue sky
green prairies, and white houses,
the scenery
from our car window
resembles a child's painting   (Central Oregon)

old eyes dazzled,
I look up at
my mixed-blood granddaughter
who has brought her boyfriend
along to visit me

did he die, then?
I gaped at the TV screen
where the death
of the panda bear, Cancan,
was being highlighted   (US NBC TV)

フイリッピン行 （マニラ）

一氣に起ち
雲表に出づ
機の横に
大きく明^{あか}し
上弦の月

^{イミグレーション}
入國管理
待たせ焦^じらせて
意味ありげに
執務する
若き顔崩さずに

ダイヤ連ねし
^{ロザリオ}
数珠に祈るは
何ならん
^{フアーストレデイ}
第一夫人
富天下に名あり

警官立つ
^{ビレジ}
村 の塀内に
家垣も
嚴しく住める
富家の人達

May Yen Ting

Going to the Philippines (Manila)

suddenly the plane rose
out of the cloud cover,
and I saw
beside us a great, bright
first quarter crescent moon

made impatient
by my enforced wait at Immigration,
I watch the young officer
work without an expression
altering his face

praying with a rosary
of diamond links,
what will she pray?
the First Lady is notorious
for her wealth on earth

inside the walled village
stands a policeman, and
the dwellings are fenced —
they live well-guarded lives,
people in these rich houses

他國土に
築きし富の
シンボルや
豪華競へる
華僑の墓園　　　　　　（華僑義山）

公園の
草屈みつつ
薙ぎ刈りゐる
どの勞務者も
早老の顔

葉に當り
地を撃ち椰子の
實の落ちし
一刹那の音
覺めゐて聞きつ

May Yen Ting

a symbol of prosperity
constructed on this foreign soil:
the unrivaled splendor
of the gardens
at the Overseas Chinese Cemetery   *(the Manila Chinese Cemetery)*

stooping over the grass
in the public park
mowing and cutting
all the workers
have prematurely aged faces

I woke up the instant
I heard the sound of a coconut
falling through the leaves
to hit the ground
with a thud

懐舊

もたらしし
友䬸に亡し
<ruby>月來香<rt>ユエライシャン</rt></ruby>
闇夜に籠る
香の咽ぶほど

ザボンの實を
木の上の母が
投げくれし
思ひ出今も
我を幼なにす

死への道

<ruby>黄金時代<rt>ゴールデンエイジ</rt></ruby>か
餘生か知らね
惻々と
限りを思ふ
我が持ち時間

Nostalgic for Old Times

the friend who brought me
this evening primrose
has already died —
the night darkness is heavy
with its suffocating fragrance

a memory of my mother
throwing down to me
a shaddock fruit
from the top of the tree – even now
that makes me feel young again

The Path to Death

not knowing whether
this is a 'golden age'
or just the rest of my life
miserably I consider the limits
of the time still left to me

非業の死
來るべくして來しか
十九年
押しに押したる
獨裁の果て　　　　　　　（韓國）

解放を
謳ひしはいつ
戰死餓死
今又萬の
確かな溺死　　　　　　（インドシナ半島）

各古屋オリンピック委員會に排斥さる

世界孤兒に
追ひ込まれつる
悲憤に堪へ
生き繼がんとす
千餘萬の民

so the violent death
that was bound to come, came—
a climactic ending
to his nineteen years
of increasingly autocratic rule   (South Korea)

when was it that
they declared 'liberation'?
deaths from war and starvation,
now a further ten thousand
confirmed dead from drowning   (the Indo-China peninsula)

Rejection by the Nagoya Olympic committee.

driven to become
orphans of the world,
countless people
endure their indignation
and try to go on living

秋の陽

高層の
窓へ「媽々！再見」と
呼ばふ學童の
聲空に散る
團地のあした

見下せる
プールの一角に
入陽射し
水面茜に
耀ひ立つる

山峽を
車の大きく
曲り來て
一望白し
芒の穗波

夜を覺めて
久々に聞きぬ
旅宿に
物叩くごと
鳴く家宮の聲

May Yen Ting

Autumn Sunshine

a school boy's voice calling
to the window of a multistory block
"see you later, Mama,"
drifts into the sky
above the morning estate

sun shines
in one corner of the pool
I'm looking down on…
it gives to the water's surface
a rosy brilliance

the car makes a big turn
around the mountain pass —
waves of white
pampas grass ears
are spread below us

I woke in the night
to something I'd not heard for a while,
the voice of a gecko
sounding like a kind of knocking
on my lodgings

ふてぶてしく

纏^{まつは}りて
襲ふ一匹の
蚊をはつしと
撲ちぬ憎しみ
やや度越えしか

庭芝の
下地を這ひて
何の木の
根ふてぶてしくも
網目を張れり

苦悩

兩強の
陣取りか相手
イランの火に
泥^{なづ}むやすかさず
アフガンを奪取す

Impudently

sharply, I slapped at
the mosquito following me
to attack—
maybe my enmity
has become excessive

creeping under the lawn
the roots of what tree
impudently
spreading its net
through the garden

Suffering

will both powers now
take up their positions?
will the opponent, Iran,
stick to its guns and
immediately seize Afghanistan?

カーター氏感恩祭に人質の無事釋放を祈る

萬策盡き
カーター氏天主に
額づくや
アラーにひれ伏す
民を向うに

Mr. Carter prays for the safe release of personnel, at the Day of Obligation Observances.

exhausting a multitude of schemes,

Mr. Carter

makes obeisance to the Emperor

in front of people who

prostrate themselves before Allah

1980-1981

立命への道

散歩道
先駆けしては
我を待つ
野犬よ垂れ毛
襤褸に似たる

音たつる
夜明けの雨に
まま聞ゆ
木の上に鳥の
幼な鳴き聲

明治生まれは今、日本全人口の八パーセントとか
明治生まれ
その稀少にも
我在るや
心おのづと
愼まんとす

彈みつけ
寝起きの床を
一氣に上ぐ
今日の恙なきを
確かめにつつ

The Path of Fate

galloping ahead
on the footpath
then waiting for me:
a stray dog with long wild hair
like a mop of rags

as dawn is breaking
amid the sound of rain
from time to time
I hear the cheeping
of young birds in the tree tops

Those born in the Meiji Era currently form 8% of the entire Japanese population, I hear.

realizing I am among
the rare few born in the Meiji Era,
and still alive,
naturally I'll try
to take care of myself

I bounce up
and put away all the bedding
at one go,
while checking to see if
I'm in good health today

立命の
道とならばや
一つづつ
追ひ上げて行く
身邊整理

海底に
岩根と在らな
命終は
かかづらはるる
なき冥々裡

來世又
此の妻娶り
指揮者<ruby>コンダクター</ruby>たらん
ポツパ氏宣らすも
顏輝かせ　　　　　　　　　（歌劇團老指揮者、妻はその歌手）

if this is where
my fate lies,
I will continue
to pursue it step by step
settling my affairs in order

when my life has ended,
let me become a rock
on the sea bottom —
better not to worry about
the great unknown

in the next world
I will be a conductor again,
and marry this same wife,
Mr. Popper announces,
his face beaming   *(the elderly conductor of an opera company with which*
his wife sings)

五十年の婚

足どりの
たゆたひにつつ
ゴールインせしか
二人三脚
五十年の婚

父母の命
唯々と嫁し來て
今日逢ふや
子孫ら集ひ
金婚の宴

May Yen Ting

Fifty Years of Marriage

with wavering gait

have we achieved our aim?

two people

in a three-legged race,

fifty years of marriage

having married

in obedience to my parents,

today I shall meet

my children and grandchildren gathering

for our Golden Wedding banquet

Afterword

In the autumn of 1971, I was fortunate to become a student of Shiga-sensei and start to learn *tanka*. I was well beyond the age of 60, the so-called "age to start to learn calligraphy." Thereafter, I enthusiastically worked on ten *tanka* each month as if to fill up the missing time between Shiga-sensei and myself since the Kantō Earthquake.

In the summer of 1975, Shiga-sensei, who was past the age of 90, encouraged me to organize the *tanka* of the previous three years. With the selection of *tanka* by Shiga-sensei, and the editing and arranging of publication by Ōta Seikyū-sensei, my first collection of *tanka*, *Destiny*, came about.

Soon after, I was at a total loss facing the sudden death of Shiga-sensei. I tried to encourage myself to work hard independently. I sent my *tanka* to *Chō-On Magazine*, through Seikyū-sensei and Ayako-sensei [絢子先生], with little confidence that it would be selected for publication.

At the end of 1979, I felt that I was at a dead end as an author/writer. Also, I felt that I had not done anything to arrange my personal matters properly. I decided to take a break from writing *tanka* and mentioned to Seikyū-sensei that I would temporarily stop writing *tanka* in 1980. Until then, I had never missed turning in my *tanka* on time.

I privately disclosed to Uematsu Setsuko-sama [植松節子様] and Kawanishi Umeko-sama [川西うめ子様] that I would gather up the *tanka* written after *Destiny* to make up a second collection. My plan was to make the second collection a milestone of my life and to commemorate our 50th wedding anniversary in 1981. I am impulsive and usually do things on a whim, but I wanted to set a goal to push myself to complete the project. If I could finish this project, anything that came after would be a bonus for me, and I could enjoy a more relaxed life.

Around April, I started to organize the *tanka*. I wrote down all the *tanka* side by side on paper, and all the shortcomings in them appeared. I realized that I had not studied hard enough, and there was no progress in my *tanka*.

While I was in Tokyo, on May 26, Uematsu Setsuko-sama took me to Kamakura to visit Seikyū-sensei and Ayako-sensei. I asked them for help with my collection of *tanka*. Though they were very busy getting ready to visit China, they agreed to help. The title, *Two Countries*, was also selected at this time from the *tanka*:

> *put bluntly,*
>
> *is this 'sitting on the fence'?*
>
> *I feel guilty*
>
> *picking and choosing*
>
> *between two countries to live in*

Here, I would like to express my sincere appreciation to Seikyū-sensei. In addition to his work on my first collection of *tanka*, he agreed to write a foreword, edit my work, and do everything involved in publishing this second collection of *tanka*.

Also, my thanks go to Uematsu-sama and Kawanishi-sama for their encouragement and great assistance.

Ting Yen May

Figure 3 – The celebration of the 50th Wedding Anniversary and Ting Ruey-Iang's 77th Birthday with the entire family of 23: three sons, two daughters, their spouses, six grandsons and five granddaughters. July 12, 1980 at the house in Portland, Oregon.

Two Countries

266

May Yen Ting

The Road to Japanese Language

Merely for the reason of my yearning for Shiga-sensei, I jumped into *Chō-On Sha* to start learning *tanka*. I was born in 1907 (明治 [Meiji] 40) in Jieh Yu Kun [鯪魚坑] of Keelung [基隆] County. Jieh Yu Kun is the Taiwanese name for *ayu* (sweetfish). Perhaps the place is so named because people were able to catch *ayu* in the Keelung River in the old days.

About 150 years ago, my forebears, great-grandfather and grandfather, moved from Anshi [安西], Fukien [福建] to Taiwan. They moved around from the middle of Taiwan to northern Taiwan in order to avoid natural disasters as well as man-made disasters, and then finally settled down in this place which had gold mines and coal mines nearby. With a clan of around fifty people, they began to cultivate the land. Also, they panned gold from the sand of the Keelung River and mined the coal of Suh Jiao Ting [四脚亭]. Their life gradually stabilized and my grandfather became well-known as a representative of the people of the area.

I was born in a house with a mountain at the back, facing the clear Keelung River in front, and guarded by large maple trees on both sides. I enjoyed my life at a very young age in this wild natural setting, catching shrimp and crabs, and climbing trees until we moved to Keelung in 1912 (大正 [Taisho] 1).

My uncle had left the group family to develop the gold and coal mining businesses earlier. Later, my father formally joined him, and our family moved. We turned from farm kids into city kids, but I made many excursions to play in the small streams and little hills while helping to take care

267

of my younger brothers and sisters who came along one after another.

In 1915 (大正 3), I entered a public school (a school for Taiwanese as opposed to the elementary schools which were only for Japanese people). I had never learned how to study, and my parents never bothered me about studying. I do not recall ever untying the big cloth-wrapped bundle of textbooks at home.

I knew a few phrases of Japanese but was unable to connect them to express complete ideas. At the end of fourth grade, my level of Japanese language proficiency was such that I could not comprehend mathematical word problems. I tried to do the problems without reading the questions, by just adding or subtracting the numbers that appeared in the questions.

The house in Keelung was a Western-style three-story house. The front half of the house was set up as office space. The families of my uncle and my father occupied the back half.

My uncle, Yen Yung-Nien [顏雲年], was born in 1874 (明治 7). He attended a private school run by my grandfather's younger brother from the age of eight. He was preparing for the Chin Dynasty [清朝] national government examination for officials when Taiwan was ceded to Japan through the signing of the Treaty of Shimonoseki [下関條約].

Soon, the Japanese army landed at Audi [澳底], not far from Keelung. The Japanese military forces gradually moved inland and even set up a guard camp at Ruifang [瑞芳] which was very close to the gold and coal mines. Rumors were rampant, and people were uneasy. And there were also some riots.

One day, the Yen family received a summons from the Japanese government. The whole family was in a panic. After much discussion among the family elders, they decided to send my uncle at the age of twenty-two to represent the Yen family. All by himself, he went to face the commander of Ruifang garrison for an interview. It turns out the order was for him to be the point of contact for communications between the Japanese government and the civilian populace. Though still young, with wisdom, enthusiasm and courage, my uncle assessed the situation and understood his mission. He decided to make an effort to assimilate. Soon after, my uncle left our old dwelling and moved his small family to Ruifang. He learned Japanese very quickly and tried his best to harmonize the relationship between the local Japanese and Taiwanese. His personal abilities and his mastery of Japanese language gradually came to be recognized and trusted.

Meanwhile, there was an influx of Japanese enterprises that wanted to explore this new world. Fujita-Kumi [藤田組], organized by the wealthy Osaka Baron Fujita, was looking for a sub-contractor to mine Jin Shan [金山, gold mountain] in Ruifang. My uncle was recommended as the most suitable person. This was the establishment of the relationship with Fujita-Kumi. Four years later, in 1903 (明治 36), the Fifth National Industrial Exhibition was held in Osaka. Not yet thirty years old, and once just a farm boy, my uncle went to Osaka with a knowledgeable developer. Through an introduction, he met a giant of the business world, the so-called man of the generation, Baron Fujita Denzaburō [藤田伝三郎]. The Baron saw my uncle's wisdom and his spirit of perseverance, and imparted to him the keys to success in life. My uncle was also able to enjoy the patronage of Baron Fujita's eldest son, Baron Fujita Heisaburo [藤田平三郎]. Because of this special connection, when the mining operation of Jin Shan in Ruifang became unprofitable, Fujita-Kumi released the operation to my uncle from among a large field of candidates. With his unique successful management skills, my uncle continued to expand his mining operations.

In 1910 (明治 43), the construction of Keelung Harbor began. My uncle foresaw that the maritime industry would be the major force behind all other industries, and coal mining would be an important factor. He started to apply for permits for mining coal in northern districts ahead of others. When he obtained the permits, he asked my father to be responsible for all the coal mining business, and he devoted himself to the gold mining business. At the time, my father was helping the head of our families, my grandfather's brother, and ran the small coal mining operations of three generations. My uncle displayed his talent and skill in business planning and in finance management of the whole group. That was why the house was built in Keelung, and we moved from Jieh Yu Kun to Keelung to live with my uncle's family.

In the first year of Taisho [大正], my uncle purchased a house in Take-baya-chō [竹早町], Koishikawa-ku [小石川區] in Tokyo and sent his three sons there to attend elementary and high school. He often stayed in Tokyo for business, and in order to get acquainted with all classes of people of Japan, and to understand the trends of the business world.

When I completed my 4th grade of public school in Taisho 7, my uncle told me to go to Tokyo to study. It was a bolt from the blue sky for both my parents and myself. A girl to go all the way to Tokyo to study! At the time, we had a couple of maids to help out, but I was a good helper for my mother taking care of my younger brothers and sisters. My father had great respect for my uncle who was 12 years his senior. My uncle had the foresight to launch various businesses and was very successful, so there was no disagreement with his ultra-progressive ideas, which changed my life and my destiny 180 degrees.

I was not that familiar with Japanese language. In the Japanese room on the third floor, with the help of the wives of some Japanese employees, I opened up my arms to let them put on Japanese undergarments, layer by layer, and a violet-tinted *kimono*. Paired with *tabi* and *zori*, suddenly I became a Japanese figure and went to Tokyo.

I was born as the head of many, many siblings and was not used to clinging to my mother. Once, someone said to my mother that it must be very hard to keep that many children well-behaved; my mother responded that if you trained the first one to behave, all the others would follow. I thought that she was a cold-hearted person to treat me in such a way. I was young and ignorant, and I did not know any differently.

I was not an overly protected child even though I lived in a big house with maids, and people referred to me as a child of so-and-so. My mother was very strict.

In April, the new school year had begun, and I entered Rekisen Elementary School [礫川小学校] near my house on Takebaya-chō. Due to the differences in standards between elementary and public schools, I was forced to repeat the fourth grade. The school had been previously attended by Taiwanese students, so I was not regarded as odd by other students. The first and second classes of Reading, titled "Sending off at Sakurai Station [櫻井駅]," in older Japanese writings was very difficult. I could not comprehend a thing. I could not raise my hand even once while other students were raising their hands without hesitation. The others could understand, and I could not. I was struck by the lonely feeling of being left out and being isolated. What if I could understand and be like the others? Unconsciously, this became my springboard to study hard. During the second term of fourth grade, we moved to Shinhana-chō [新花町], Yushima [湯島], Hongō-ku [本郷區]. I transferred to the Hongō Motomachi [元町] Elementary School. I was the first "foreign" student to attend the school. I felt others staring at me with strange looks. I felt lonely and sad at the time. One day, I went home for lunch. Lunch was delayed because my uncle had visitors. By the time I rushed back to school, the main gate was closed since the class had already begun. I could not find the small gate that allowed entry in this type of situation since I was new to the school. I went home dejectedly instead. The next morning, the classmate sitting next to me apologized saying, "I am sorry. We talked about you behind your back." I tried to find out what was going on then. It turned out that my teacher had spoken with my class and told them that the reason I was absent was because of all of the talk behind my back. The class was instructed to be kind to me. I was unable to explain the truth behind my absence from school that afternoon, and I felt bad for my classmates.

My Japanese was still not perfect, but I had made great progress, and I was able to get by. Once, in a sewing class, I asked my teacher to return part of a sleeve of the garment to me. "Return the *so-re* [それ] to me." The teacher did not understand. "What is it?" she asked me repeatedly. I knew my face was getting red. The classmates around us were also noisily talking about us. Finally, the teacher said, "Oh, you mean *so-de* [そで]?" I was flustered; I was not able to distinguish the sound of *"da"* [だ] from *"ra"* [ら] and *"de"* [で] from *"re"* [れ].

From then on, I paid special attention to pronunciation and became very precise in my speech.

Around 1919 (大正 8), the admissions rate to high school from elementary school became an important issue. Starting from the fifth grade, classes were organized as follows: a co-ed class, a class of all boys, and a class of all girls. It was rumored that the co-ed class would be formed from students with better records. It was the so-called "entrance exam group." Fortunately, I was placed in this class. After regular school hours, we remained for an extra two hours to study the most emphasized subjects. The male teacher had faith and passion for a rigorous education. The teaching was strict but filled with emotion, and all the students eagerly followed him. There was a lot of homework. Writing essays was the most difficult task for me. What should I write? There were two maids at home. I got some hints from them and sought help in the indirect expression of writing. I gradually got the hang of it. Some of the better works were returned to me with the teacher's markings. I rewrote a clean copy of them and turned them in again. This time, the works were printed on the mimeographed straw paper and were distributed among the students as an article of appreciation. To me, it was an incentive, and writing gradually became a non-issue. As the entrance examination of the girls' high school approached, the teacher was worried about the level of my Japanese language and gave me private lessons after school. He offered instruction on how to answer the questionnaire after reading of two or three lessons of the textbook.

I went to see the posting of the list of successful candidates at Tokyo Prefectural First Girls' High School. When I saw my number, I was so happy that I grabbed the hands of an unknown candidate and just kept jumping up and down. Only after boarding the train for home, did I notice that I had lost a couple of buttons from my coat.

By entering this school, I was connected with Shiga-sensei. With a smiling face, a large and full bosom, to a girl like me who had left a home far away, she projected an image of mother's love. I felt that she was really nice.

Her teaching of "National Literature" in a one- or two-hour class, impressed every student. One day, after entering the high school, I told my friends playfully, "The shoes were polished [*migaite kudasatta*, みがいて くださった] by my maid." One of my friends told me, "Gan-San, you should say polished [*migaite kureta*, みがいて くれた]." I could never understand the reason that my friend corrected me. I even thought she was teasing me. Everyday, I learned something new, and I was acquiring more knowledge. I felt I was growing very rapidly, and the gap between me and other students was narrowing. My life at school was very happy.

A few of us drew pictures, wrote essays, and wrote poetry and made a bound book, which we circulated around and enjoyed. Around this time, I started to feel the rhythm of *haiku* and *tanka* and thought they were interesting and special. Borrowing the forms, I wrote poetry to tease or banter back and forth with my friends for fun. Today, I do not remember what I wrote or even if they were in the form of *haiku* or *tanka*. I recall that I had a notebook filled up with my poems. An old teacher, who lived with us and supervised us and taught us to read and count, thought it was a strange work and took me to visit his fellow town folks to review the book. In only two and half years of school life before the Kantō Earthquake, I learned a great deal. After transferring to the Taipei First Girls' High School, a four-year system school, and graduating from it, I was able to enter the Tokyo Women's Higher Normal College (today's Ochanomizu University). I credit that to the strong foundation of learning that I received from that Tokyo Prefectural First Girls' High School.

Reflecting on the past, my uncle grabbed unthinkable opportunities during the time that Japan ruled Taiwan. He contacted Japan ahead of others, and tried to understand Japan and sense global trends, courageously connecting Taiwan and Japan as asked. He took it as his mission to harmonize the relationship between Taiwan and Japan, and he took the lead in its execution.

At the time, he dealt with the Japanese enterprises that came to Taiwan and their able employees with masterful Japanese language. My uncle had only been tutored in classical Chinese at a private school (*juku*). His character was cultivated very rapidly in every phase, and he had become a grown man.

These are the factors that led to the trust and patronage of two generations of Baron Fujita. He was able to acquire the full rights to mine and became a leader of the industry. He also expanded businesses jointly managed by the Mitsui family.

My uncle loved poetry. His love for poetry may have come from his study of Han literature for the official governmental examinations at private school in the Chin Dynasty before Japan ruled Taiwan. He called himself "Singing Dragon" and named his firstborn girl, Poem. He chaired poetry associations and held many readings of poetry at his homes in both Tokyo and Taiwan. While I was living in Yushima Shinhana-chō, my room was close to my uncle's room. Sometimes, the loud recitation of poems would stop suddenly, and then the sound of an abacus would come through. I thought that my uncle was strange. Upon reading his short biography, I understood that poetry meant as much to him as his business. It was not a small thing for him. To him, poetry not only enhanced his mining business but also gave him room to breathe.

In 1917 (大正 6), a big dispute broke out regarding mining rights between Count Yoshikawa Kanji [伯爵芳川寛治] and my uncle. Yoshikawa betrayed my uncle's trust. It was the biggest setback of his life. He wrote a poem in the "Hyo-Lin Style [評林体]" to release his deep regrets and melancholy.

Visited Tokyo nine times in three years

Do not mind the hard work for mining rights

Do not laugh at my mistakes made when I was young

Now I am more mature and know to do better

Take my in-house dispute as a national matter

My plan is clear to save Han by surrounding Chao

To cut the chicken or rabbit with a heavy hatchet

Will not mind about the onlookers laughing

High power pressure is as heavy as a mountain

Have a plan to return the jade intact

After all - overpowering force used is futile

Truth still upheld among people

There is a thick coal mine in Jin Bao Li

Aggressively fighting for the assets in Suh Jiao Ting

Gained an inch and looked for a foot

Wild cat effortlessly coveting the smell of fish

(Jin Bao Li [金包里] and Suh Jiao Ting were the locations of the coal mines)

Playing Chinese chess was also one of my uncle's hobbies.

After being betrayed by Yoshikawa, my uncle kept a low profile for a time. Then, with his spirit of perseverance and with his wisdom, he started to plan to counter Yoshikawa. Quickly and quietly, he started to buy up the shares of the mining company that Yoshikawa chaired. The number of shares he purchased was close to Yoshikawa's. Just before he was ready to confront Yoshikawa, the dispute was settled through some middleman. In his short biography, he described how he tried to counter Yoshikawa using the steps of a chess game. I could imagine the face of my uncle playing chess with my cousins vividly. He foresaw the trends of social affairs as he foresaw the moves of a chess game, and planned his business accordingly, step by step. He also applied his hobbies of poetry and chess to his business operations and became a successful mining operator, I must say.

My uncle respected the art of living. He protected the family principles and followed the family discipline of frugality. But he loved beautiful things and enjoyed the aesthetics of them. He would incorporate them into his life without hesitation. At the end of the Meiji Era, when I was three or four years old, he was already using elegant Japanese teacups and lacquered chopsticks. One time when I was his guest, I liked them so much that I put a pair of chopsticks in my pocket and refused to give them up. The cup was too big to put in my pocket. My aunt promised to give me a pair of chopsticks and a teacup when I returned to Jieh Yu Kun, and I finally let them go to be washed. Dressed in a *kimono* and *hakama*, my uncle looked the very image of the olden days' description of a very handsome young man. My aunt wore her Taiwanese-style dress with her hair in a bun looking lovely.

In 1919 (大正 8), a Japanese garden was built near the Kimura Shrine. My uncle liked it so much that he, with my father, proceeded to purchase the garden from Kimura Kyutaro [木村久太郎] who was my uncle's partner in running the coal mine. My father built a western-style house and lived at one end of the garden. My uncle occupied the Japanese-style mansion. From the main living room, he was able to view the pond. Also, beyond the pond, he was able to enjoy the various colors of azaleas on the slope. In autumn, he enjoyed the blooming chrysanthemums which had been brought in from Japan and cultivated by a few gardeners. Further, he left it open to the public and shared his joy of it with the people of Keelung. Keelung did not have a park-like park at that time, and it naturally became a destination for the citizens of Keelung to walk to, and it was also a nice playground for children.

Legend says that one famous Yen ancestor, Yen Hui, lived on a "shabby lane," so my uncle named this park "Shabby Garden [陋園]." Of course, youngsters were unaware of the origin of the name and called it the "Garden of Yen Guo-Nien [顏國年]" after my father. My uncle selected ten scenes in the garden and wrote poems describing them. During World War II, some military installations were placed in the garden and when the war intensified, it was bombed until there was nothing left. It had been one of the most famous spots in Keelung, and the large meeting room had been used for many public events.

Yoshikawa, who had betrayed my uncle by breaking the mediated agreement, eventually turned over all the mining rights to the Mitsui [三井] family. That was in 1918 (大正 7). The Mitsui and Yen families formed the Keelung Coal Mining Corporation and started a new era of cooperation.

My husband, Ting Ruey-Iang, who graduated from Tokyo University of Commerce [東京商科大字, today's Hitotsubashi University (現一橋大學)] in 1917 (大正 7), joined this company upon graduation and worked in the area of labor relations for 17 years. After the war, the company was taken over by the Chinese government. My husband decided to leave the Yen family business to seek his own destiny, even though my eldest cousin, who was in charge of all Yen family businesses, offered him a position leading the gold mine operations.

In 1923 (大正 12), at the end of December, my uncle finished a meeting with Mitsui Mining and boarded a ship heading for Taiwan. He felt uncomfortable on the ship. He worked without rest through the end of the year. He fell ill as the new year arrived. Was it malaria? In addition to local doctors, doctors from the Mitsui family, and doctors across from the Yushima Shinhana-chō house, Dr. Irizawa [入沢博士] was sent to examine him. It turned out to be typhoid, too late to cure. He died just as he reached the age of 50.

My father was 38 then. Following the wishes of my uncle, he took over the operations of the whole business, and he became the guardian of my cousins. Though they were brothers, my father was quite different from my uncle. He had a different character and approached work differently. My father had a smiling and approachable round face, and he was gentle, upright and passionate. Regarding business, he was very cautious and thought through matters in depth. He was considered to be very sharp with numbers. My uncle had a square face that commanded the respect. He was strong and daring, an intelligent type. He dealt business with aggressiveness and courage. He was full of wisdom. People perceived that my uncle was creative and venturesome while my father was conservative and would keep the status quo. This combination made them a successful pair of business-men. My father appeared to either not be interested at all or not have time for hobbies since he worked day and night. He was good at deck golf which he played and enjoyed on the ship between Taiwan and Japan. To reporters, he was not at all interested in art or metaphysical issues, but he was deeply attracted to new innovations in machinery, new plant layouts, and matters related to business management.

Someone once said that my poems were realistic. It could very well be that I inherited my father's blood. My father talked a lot about numbers. My secret assessment of my father was that he was a forthright man. Once, we took a boat down stream on Tama River [多摩川] and had a lunch at a Japanese restaurant. My father took out a notebook in an alcove and wrote a poem on the spot. That was when I realized that my father could write poetry. He was not that serious about it, but when inspired, he could compose without a problem.

The world economy was in chaos from 1929 to 1934 (昭和 4 to 9). Businesses were depressed, and my father had a very hard time managing the business. He had, in the past, visited mining operations all over the world and learned how to manage the business efficiently and to improve the operations. After the business turned around and the future began to look bright, at the age of 52, in 1937 (昭和 12), my father had a stroke and passed away. Later, his will was found in the drawer of his desk. It had been written when he was 50.

My uncle and my father did not learn their Japanese through any formal education. They learned it through listening and memorizing. They were able to communicate ideas, but their pronunciations were not quite accurate. My father occasionally asked me about the pronunciation of words when he was asked to read public statements.

My father was kind and granted almost all of my requests. I can still see the image of my younger brothers, taking turns, placing their heads on my father's lap, on the *tatami*, getting their ears cleaned.

On the island of Takasago

With a tint of Yamato

Full blossoms of a cherry tree

Sadly fallen

This was the message of condolence offered by Yoshida Tsutomu for my father.

It evokes the image of my father, who was gentle and upright, full of humanity, following the path of my uncle.

My mother was brought up on a tea farm. During the tea leaf picking season, while maintaining the household, she was taught to sew simple materials by my grandmother when she was five or six years old. Sewing was her special skill. Marrying into a big family of farmers, her duty was to cook for everybody. If it was not her turn to cook, she was tasked to clean the rice for the whole extended family. She was young and was mostly assigned to cook during the busiest harvest season. With children arriving continuously, and with the workload of feeding, sewing, and laundering, every day was a hard day. While working, she had a child bound to her back. There was a story that she did not realize that a child had learned to walk. When she put down the child to feed him milk, the child walked away from her. After moving to Keelung, her workload was reduced but since her milk had dried out, she had a very difficult time providing the children with enough nutrition. While they were living in Jieh Yu Kun, there was no public health organization. Childbirth would be handled most often by an experienced, older person. I heard that my aunt assisted in my birth. Thereafter, my mother herself handled the births of the subsequent children. After moving to Keelung, doctors and midwives were readily available. However, she was accustomed to it, so she handled the childbirths herself.

While she was in the middle of washing clothes, before we knew it, she was done with giving birth, and back moving around again. My mother was a strong-willed person. She was a diligent hard worker, and a person of forbearance. It was the age before ready-made clothing. The clothes we wore, including school uniforms, and my father's suits and his tailcoat, were all handmade by my mother. She often mentioned that on average, large or small, she made several tens of articles of clothing a month. There was no education system when my mother was born. She was self-taught and used an abacus to keep the household accounting. She asked my father about the Chinese characters in the book, *Thousands of Poems*. Later, attending a Japanese class, she copied difficult phrases onto paper and pasted them near the sewing machine and tried to memorize them while she was sewing. When my father passed away, she entered a life of total immersion in religion. She spent her old age reciting Buddhist scriptures daily and prepared for the end of her life. In 1955, she passed away at the age of 69.

Blessed with the fortune created by the hard work of my uncle, my father and my mother in business and at home, I was able to enjoy the carefree life of a young girl and my youthful days in Tokyo. Just like there is a mountain there, Tokyo Women's Higher Normal College was near my home in Yushima, and I just enrolled. Since I had entered the school without any purpose, I felt the atmosphere of the school to be gloomy. I did not study very hard. I went to see movies and attended shows at the theater. I spent a lot of time attending events that I did not learn anything for myself. Four years passed. I was not stimulated to write a poem or two, and I let the classes on *banyo*, *kokon*, and new *kokon* just pass through my ears. There was a lecture by an old teacher on Chinese poetry. At the time, I thought that had nothing to do with me, so I did not even bother to listen. Thinking back, I was just an ignorant young girl. Since I was in the literary department and had spent four years in the dormitory fully immersed in Japanese, I was given the qualification to teach Japanese language and Japanese literature. I became a teacher at Keelung Girls' High School. More than ninety percent of the students were Japanese.

Since I did not use Taiwanese, it became rusty and remained at the level I had in my childhood. I was unable to communicate my feelings or ideas to my parents freely. One of my worries in my youth was the inability to communicate with my parents fully.

For two years before and after I got married, while standing on a platform in a classroom, I began to realize the importance of my teaching job. My teaching methods might not have been quite mature, but I connected with the students with all my heart. I left teaching because I did not have the confidence that I could do well both at school and at home. I became an "education-minded mother" and spent all my energy on my five children.

Before the end of the war, my children attended the same school that Japanese attended in order for them to learn perfect Japanese. My thinking was that in order for the children feel comfortable in school, they must be "good students." I was too eager for success and before I knew it, my method of educating children became the teaching of my own views. Perhaps that caused some of my children to lose their own initiative. Then the Chinese came and replaced the Japanese school system. The children were confused, and I was confused. Some were able to follow the new guidelines, and some were not. In the end, without knowing what to do, I recalled that I had been sent to Tokyo without any of my own initiative, and it suddenly struck me: at the time, a few students had begun going abroad to the United States to study, so I thought about sending my children to America. One child, who had not considered it before, took my suggestion and flew away. Then, one by one, all my children flew away following his example. Now they are all settled in America, which is one of the reasons that I go back and forth between Taiwan and America.

After all my children had left, I thought about my situation and pondered what I should do. I did not have any skills except that I had been a teacher at one time. I thought about teaching Japanese, which I had spent a long time learning. While teaching at a private college, I decided to help those young men who knew nothing about Japan understand the real and true Japan. During nearly eight years of teaching, I published two books of Japanese readings, grammar of spoken language, and Japanese conversations. Thinking that these textbooks would be available for students who wanted to learn Japanese, I stopped teaching.

I decided to do things that I wished I could have done but that I had never done. *Haiku* or *tanka* started to float in front of me like a dream. Which should I pick? I was at a loss and could not make up my mind when I met Uematsu Setsuko-sama. She told me that Shiga-sensei was her aunt.

I jumped at the chance to work with Shiga-sensei without hesitation. Not only was I not too late; a collection of my *tanka* was published under her supervision. I am the most fortunate person in the world. The two countries referenced in the title are Japan, which I love with all my heart in the past and present, and Taiwan, where I now live. In addition, it refers to Mainland China that I always had in mind and Taiwan.

The calligraphy for the cover of *Two Countries* were written by my husband Ting Ruey-Iang just as he did for my book, *Destiny*.

My husband graduated from Tainan School of Commerce [台南商專], Taipei Higher Commercial School [台北高商] and Tokyo University of Commerce. Naturally, he is a total outsider to the world of *tanka*.

However, he has always been helpful for my works of *tanka*. I have been very fortunate.

Ting Yen May
End of July, 1981
Portland, Oregon

About the Author

Ting Yen May was born in Taiwan during the Japanese Occupation. At the age of eleven, she was sent to Tokyo for schooling. She overcame her language deficiencies and successfully completed high school in Japan and became the first Taiwanese to graduate from Ochanomizu University. She learned Mandarin Chinese after the end of World War II and the end of the Japanese Occupaton. In her late fifties, she taught Japanese at Tatung College of Technology [大同工學院] and wrote several Japanese language textbooks. She began writing Japanese poetry (*tanka*) in her sixties after reconnecting with her high school teacher/mentor who guided and encouraged her in publishing *Destiny*, her first book of *tanka*. *Two Countries* is her second collection of *tanka*. Ting Yen May's creative ability and perseverance in overcoming every obstacle led to her success in life.

About the Translator

Amelia Fielden, an Australian, is a professional translator of Japanese literature, specializing in the translation of *tanka* poetry. She is also an internationally published and awarded poet writing *tanka* in English.

Amelia gained a Bachelor of Asian Studies (Japanese Honors) degree from the Australian National University and holds a post-graduate diploma in Modern Japanese Translation and a Master of Arts (Japanese Literature).

Over the last twenty years, 24 books of Amelia's *tanka* translations have been published. These include work by poet Kawano Yuko, English collaborations with other poets, bilingual *tanka* anthologies, and her own original poetry, the latest being 'These Purple Years.'

Amelia is an active member of the Limestone Poets (Australia), The Tanka Society of America, and the International Tanka Society.

www.ingramcontent.com/pod-product-compliance
Lightning Source LLC
Chambersburg PA
CBHW060005100426
42740CB00010B/1400